what your dog wants

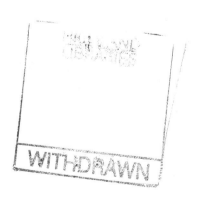

what
your
dog
wants

hamlyn

KAREN WILD

An Hachette UK Company
www.hachette.co.uk

First published in
Great Britain in 2012 by
Hamlyn, a division of
Octopus Publishing Group Ltd
Endeavour House
189 Shaftesbury Avenue
London WC2H 8JY
www.octopusbooks.co.uk

ISBN 9780600624639

A CIP catalogue record for this
book is available from the British
Library

Printed and bound in China

10 9 8 7 6 5 4 3 2 1

Acknowledgements

Executive editor: Trevor Davies
Designed and produced by SP Creative Design
Editor: Heather Thomas
Designer: Rolando Ugolini
Special photography: Rolando Ugolini

The author would like to thank Martin Gadd and all her
colleagues at the Association of Pet Behaviour Counsellors.

Picture credits
The publishers would like to thank: Bez Bakinowska,
Sara Bell, Marcia and John Castle, Hannah Howard,
Kamila Page, Jane Robson, Phil Sime and Linda Williams.

Octopus Publishing Group Limited/Rolando Ugolini 8, 11,
13, 14, 16 top, 18 bottom, 19, 20, 21 bottom, 23 left, 24,
25, 28, 29, 30, 31, 32, 33, 34, 35, 37, 38 top, 42, 43, 44,
45, 46, 47, 48 top, 50, 51, 52, 53, 54 top, 55, 56 top, 58,
59, 63, 64, 65, 67 top, 73, 75 bottom, 78, 79 bottom, 81,
84, 86, 95

Octopus Publishing Group Limited/Russell Sadur 10, 38
bottom, 40, 56, 61, 62, 66, 70, 74, 75 top

Rolando Ugolini 7, 9, 12, 15, 16 bottom, 18 top, 18
middle, 21 top, 22, 23 right, 39, 41, 48 bottom, 49, 54
bottom, 57, 60, 69 bottom, 72, 76, 77, 79 top, 80, 82,
83, 85, 88, 89, 90, 91, 92, 93, 94

SP Creative Design 17, 26, 27, 67 bottom, 68, 69 top, 71, 87

Contents

Introduction

Knowing what your dog wants is one of the greatest skills you can develop as a caring, responsible owner. As we spend so much time with our canine companions, we owe it to them to learn everything we can about their behaviour. By developing and using the seven key skills, together with the training exercises, which are featured in this book, you and your dog can develop an even closer bond and have a more rewarding relationship.

Throughout the progression and life stages from puppy to elderly dog, comparing breed differences and temperament variations, as well as discovering the science of canine body language and interactions, helps you to share your dog's view of the world. And the simple-to-follow training sections provide an essential training toolkit, so you can transform your dog into a responsive and obedient family pet.

Health considerations are extremely important, along with understanding your dog's wellbeing, both physical and mental. Providing the correct care and exercise has to be balanced with keeping your dog mentally stimulated in a way that only he can appreciate. Owning a dog is an enormous responsibility – more so now than ever before as our dogs are expected to behave impeccably at all times but especially in public. It is incumbent upon you to become your dog's human guardian and keep him safe, not only within the confines of your own home and garden but also when you're out and about together, and this book tells you how.

The emphasis throughout is on the positive and enjoyable aspects of owning a dog, always using kind, fair and effective methods, which are explained in detail. Teamwork is key to building a satisfying and rewarding relationship for both of you. Your dog is only with you for a relatively short time compared to the average human lifespan, and he will repay your efforts with so much devotion, pleasure and companionship. In return, you must ensure that you give him everything he needs for a healthy and contented life. Understanding what your dog wants and developing the seven key skills of good dog ownership to deliver it has never been so enjoyable!

SKILL
LEVEL

Skill 1: Comprehension

Dogs have a unique way of expressing themselves and give many posture signals. By observing these, you can learn how they view their environment and, more importantly, you and the rest of their human family. By developing these essential skills, you can learn to read your dog and discover how dogs relate to each other by looking for the behaviour patterns they exhibit.

Canine senses

Dogs have abilities far superior to those of humans where their senses are concerned. Your dog will see, hear, smell or feel situations differently to you. This knowledge helps you control, understand and teach him far more simply.

Visual skill

A dog's visual field varies according to type or breed and how close together his eyes are – those with longer muzzles usually have a greater field of vision. Dogs are also expert at detecting movement. Border Collies are extremely responsive to this – they appear drawn to movement and stare in a fixed way, enabling them to react quickly.

Hearing

Your dog hears high-pitched tones much better than you can. His hearing depends on his breed and age, but as his ears are mobile he can use them to help him locate sound. Pricked or upright, curved ears intensify sound in the same way that we might 'cup' our ears. A dog with longer ears, such as a Spaniel, will not hear so proficiently, as the ear canal is covered. Be aware of your dog's sensitivity to sound as it could affect his behaviour, especially if he dislikes some noises. Hearing is important, but deaf dogs can be trained and still make good pets.

◀ Short-nosed breeds like this Pug only have a 200-degree field of vision unlike, say, an Afghan Hound with 290-degree vision. This compares to a human's total view of around 180 degrees.

◀ Never underestimate
how your dog's excellent
sense of smell governs his
natural behaviours.

Touch

Your dog develops this sense before all others – his entire
body is covered with touch-sensitive nerve endings. Most
dogs enjoy human touch and gentle massage, especially
around their ears and the sides of the neck and chest.
Dogs must learn that humans will touch them and not
view it as a threat, even if they are very sensitive to touch.

Taste

This is the least important of dogs' senses: they have six
times fewer taste buds than us. They are located near the
tip of the tongue, but even though dogs can distinguish
sweet, bitter, sour and salty flavours, their sense of
smell is so closely linked that they probably receive more
information about food by smelling rather than tasting it.

Smell

This is the dog's most powerful skill by far. Your dog has
an extraordinary ability to detect and identify smells. He
has an incredible 220 million scent receptors compared
to our five million. Dogs have an organ known as the
vomeronasal, or Jacobson's organ, that helps them analyse
the smell even further. Their highly developed brains also
assist in sorting the array of scent information. Dogs' nose
work skills are used for search and rescue and to detect
drugs and explosives. There are even medical detection
dogs to detect cancer and help people with diabetes.

Colour

Dogs are not colour blind
– they see shades of blue,
yellow and grey – but they
have trouble distinguishing
between green, yellow,
orange and red. A red toy
that is easy for you to see
is hard for your dog to
distinguish from green
grass. This may explain
why he races past it!

How your dog sees the world

SKILL LEVEL

The closest bond between you and your dog will be formed when you see the world through his eyes. Objects and events that can appear normal and humdrum to you can have quite the opposite effect on him. The whirl of human lives, with their ever-changing social networks and material objects, can easily overwhelm a dog. Equally, although we cannot hope to appreciate the smells and textures of our surroundings in the same way as our dogs, we can develop the skill of appreciating how they view their world.

What does he want?

You may not understand why your dog eats unspeakable items or loves to roll in the faeces of other animals. Some dogs chase squirrels or cats, or jump up to greet people. These are natural behaviours for a canine, even if they are baffling to us. It is unfair to punish your dog for his attempts to meet needs that simply match his canine expectations for enjoyment. Ask yourself what your dog really wants and work towards meeting those needs within the boundaries you set for acceptable behaviour.

Resources matter

Dogs differ in the priorities they place on the resources around them. These include food, toys and locations, such as their bed or a sofa. Alternatively, they may place high value on certain people or meeting other dogs. Identify your dog's priorities as this can make for easier training and a more harmonious lifestyle. Does he gather up his toys or not release them easily? If so, teach him to swap them for food. If he favours a particular location in your house, practise calling him away for a tasty treat.

△ Acceptable behaviour for your dog might be unacceptable to humans, and should always be calmly discouraged from a very early age while a puppy is still small.

Food

Dogs have a very high desire for food and, usually, this makes them easy to teach in training classes. However, make sure it does not lead to problems with stealing food at home or even excessive weight gain. Food is a great and simple motivator, so never underestimate its power when teaching your dog to behave in the desired way.

Suitable training food is smelly, soft and tasty, such as small pieces of chicken or cheese, rather than dry biscuits. Make sure your dog is hungry before you start teaching, so that he really wants the food reward on offer.

Hunting and chasing

Dogs still have strong predatory instincts, and although pet dogs do not need to hunt for food to survive, many enjoy this activity. Chasing is addictive, so make sure that your dog is restricted to only chasing – and retrieving – objects that you can control, such as balls, toys and Frisbees, not cyclists, joggers and other dogs or livestock.

Companionship

Dogs enjoy company, and this is one of the reasons why they share our lives so successfully. They need social contact to breed with other dogs, but they play together for fun, too. Some breeds are more independent than others, such as terriers and huskies.

Stress and survival

If your dog is put under pressure, he will experience stress. He may respond by trying to get away from the situation, or he may stand his ground. If he thinks he is under threat, he is only reacting to survive. You must become familiar with his reactions and intervene early. In this way you can keep him safe and protect him from defending himself in unacceptable ways.

Dogs are different

Dogs all have their own needs and personalities, just like humans. This can vary greatly, even within the same litter of puppies. Breed differences can mean that some dogs are more similar than others in the way they think and act, but this is not guaranteed. For example, you can get laid-back terriers or scent hounds that show no natural instinct to hunt.

⬤ **Food is a simple, cheap and easy-to-control motivator to help train your dog. Be sure to reward him for good behaviour.**

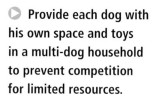

▶ **Provide each dog with his own space and toys in a multi-dog household to prevent competition for limited resources.**

Dog-to-dog relationships

SKILL
LEVEL

Your dog will come into contact with many other dogs during his life. He might even share his home with several. Like us, dogs form relationships with each other, although their needs and expressions are different. They communicate and signal to one another in ways we can learn to read. Developing this essential skill will increase your understanding of your dog's behaviour.

Saying hello

Dogs greet each other by exploring the main scent areas. They usually start by sniffing and then head for each other's rear ends, at which point they may stop, briefly shake themselves and then return. Your dog may assess another's body language long before you realize whether the other dog is approachable, so always let him make the choice.

Are they friendly?

Dogs need to mix together regularly if they are to stay sociable, and this process should start with puppy socialization and continue into adult life. Make regular play-dates for your dog with other friendly dogs, and give him the freedom to express himself. When you're out walking, be aware that a tight lead can sometimes mask or alter your dog's behaviour, so teach him not to pull towards other dogs.

🔻 **Puppies need to learn social manners if they are to develop confident adult dog relationships. Socialization and play help to develop their skills.**

Puppies and older dogs

Well-socialized older dogs will allow a puppy to do some things they would not tolerate from an adult dog, teaching a puppy gently, but firmly, if he oversteps the mark. Puppies need to learn these lessons to know how to behave in canine society. If things appear to be getting out of hand, always step in to distract both dogs gently.

🔺 **A well-socialized adult dog can teach important skills and also shows reasonable tolerance in energetic games and play, so a younger puppy is not overwhelmed.**

Does sex matter?

Dogs of both sexes play together happily, but sometimes they may have a preference. Adolescent males may not get along as readily with one another as with a female. Castration and spaying can also affect a dog's behaviour with other dogs, so always seek professional advice if you are advised to neuter your dog for behavioural reasons.

Mine, mine, mine!

Dogs do not understand the concept of sharing resources which can lead to conflict, so ensure they have plenty of toys. Divide your attention equally between them if you have more than one and give each his own food bowl. Control possessive behaviour by looking for the early warning signs, such as snatching or 'collecting' items. If you're taking an item off your dog, swap it for something better – he will learn that hands give something in return and this will relax him when they reach out towards him.

Play

Do not allow your dog to play rough games with other dogs, as he will learn how to bully them. Call him away immediately if you think that the situation is potentially stressful. If both dogs want to carry on the game, give them time to calm down and then let them play again. By doing this you stay in control of the situation.

Dog-to-human relationships

SKILL
LEVEL

Our dogs form individual relationships with each member of their human family; they learn this skill through day-to-day contact. Relationships between dogs and humans are complex, and dogs are very good at predicting what we humans will do next. They are great readers of our behaviour and moods!

Creating a bond

- Be consistent: make sure your dog knows what to expect from you – this will help to establish trust.

- Be fair: allow him to learn what to do and expect some mistakes. Give him every opportunity for success

- Be confident: he relies on you to keep him safe in the human world – this is your job as his guardian. Teach him to seek you out whenever he is unsure.

- Be responsible: he cannot always make the right choices, so be prepared to step in and take charge early if he makes a bad decision.

Socialization is key

To live in harmony, dogs must get used to humans at an early age. This process is called 'socialization'. From as early as six weeks, a puppy must start mixing with people of all ages and dispositions – tall, short, old, young, and wearing different clothes, hats and beards. If yours has not completed his vaccinations when you take him home, carry him around to socialize him. Dogs not socialized from an early age are prone to stress, fearfulness and aggression as they perceive some normal events as novel and threatening.

How dogs read humans

Dogs are expert in reading our body language – they understand facial expressions, even when reading our

▶ **It is easy for owners to communicate with their dogs by using their body language and teaching them hand signals.**

faces upside down. They also interpret our actions constantly. When interacting with your dog, try giving body signals before you speak and watch him react to even the slightest movement you make.

Human affection

We show affection in ways our dogs do not recognize as kindness. Hugging, patting and cuddling them is our way of demonstrating our love, but this may not be welcome or may even be frightening. By reading your dog's body language you will know if he feels relaxed or tense, when someone tries to touch him. If he tries to move away, offer a treat or toy, so he associates touching with having fun. Always give him a chance to move away when you stroke him. If, when you stop, he moves closer to you, he is showing you he's happy and wants you to continue.

⬤ Learning your dog's signals helps build a strong lifetime bond between you.

Who's in charge?

Gently but firmly establish ground rules for your dog. Canines are opportunists, and he will do what makes him most comfortable – he might choose the warmest place to sit, or gobble down food that is not for him. Don't get angry or confront him to get him to behave in a way you would like. Instead, show him you are in charge by training him with kind methods to do the things you want, rather than punishing him when it is too late.

Children and dogs

If dogs grow up with children they become accustomed to their noise and activity. Even if you teach your children how to handle and respect your dog, accidents still happen. Studies show that they cannot read dog body language and misinterpret what they see, such as thinking a snarling dog is 'smiling', so it is essential that adults supervise all contact between dogs and children to prevent mutual misunderstandings. Your dog may not always understand why children behave in certain ways and may be unsettled if he has not been regularly exposed to this; a child may whisper secrets into his ears, but he could perceive this as threatening behaviour.

⬤ Human signs of affection can be confusing to a dog that is not used to hugging and petting. Children find it hard to understand that dogs may not always appreciate it.

Think dog!

SKILL LEVEL

As dogs cannot talk, and usually bark only when they are very excited, as responsible owners we must learn to read their body language. The skill is to recognize the telltale signs on offer, using your dog's body posture and expressions. Sometimes these signs are deliberate, as when he is trying to tell you something, but at other times, you need to interpret his body signals to understand how he feels or reacts in a specific situation. By learning to 'think dog' you and your dog will become a true team.

Body language

Begin by looking at your dog in a range of different situations. Observe his head, mouth, eyes, tail, facial expressions and general body posture. Make a note of what is happening around him at these times, so you can better predict – and control – his reaction in the future.

Eyes

Dogs show the whites of their eyes, in a 'crescent moon' shape, if they are feeling worried or unsure. Check out any other signals and distract your dog to help him relax.

🔺 A dog experiencing stress may hide behind your legs or otherwise avoid a situation. Allow him space to explore in his own time.

▶ The early signs that your dog may be feeling unsettled can include a visible 'crescent' of white in both of his eyes.

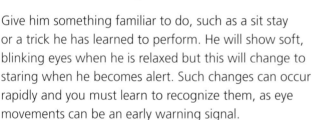

A listening dog's ears are pricked and often accompanied by a head tilt.

An alert dog's ears are upright and tilted forward. This is evident even on dogs with ears that are folded over, such as Labradors.

Give him something familiar to do, such as a sit stay or a trick he has learned to perform. He will show soft, blinking eyes when he is relaxed but this will change to staring when he becomes alert. Such changes can occur rapidly and you must learn to recognize them, as eye movements can be an early warning signal.

Ears

A dog may prick his ears up when he's alert, although this is easier to see in German Shepherds than, say, Labradors, which have folded-over ears. Dogs move their ears back when they feel relaxed, but be aware that if they are 'pinned back' it may be a sign of fear. Notice the position of your dog's ears when he experiences something new or enjoyable or worrying – they will look different at each of these stages. If his ears are pushed firmly up and forward, or pinned well back, this is an extreme reaction to a stimulus nearby, so you must take control of the situation by calling him to you.

Mouth

Your dog's mouth is highly expressive. Lips drawn back away from his teeth can be an aggressive response, but if he lifts the corners of his mouth he is relaxed. Dogs under pressure will lick around their lips and nose, and may even yawn – these are pacifying signals or early signs of stress. Many photographs of dogs show this licking and yawning behaviour as they react to having a camera pointed at them. If your dog snarls, remove him from the situation immediately or change whatever may be causing this stress. Make a note of his reaction and retrain him to cope by carrying out a process of gradual desensitization, getting him used to the stress little by little.

 Rapid nose licking can be an appeasement signal.

Head

A dog's head carriage indicates how he is feeling. If your dog averts his gaze and turns his head away he is not being rude or stubborn – he is feeling uncomfortable. However, if he lowers his head and stares in a fixed way, he is issuing a warning, usually a sign of possessive behaviour over toys or food. If you teach him that food and toys are plentiful, he will relax his body language by raising his head. He may also 'twist' his head from side to side to help him locate sounds.

 One ear may rotate if a dog feels uncomfortable.

 A mildly stressed dog will avert his head and you will see the crescent of white showing in his eyes. His tail will be tucked under and his ears slightly back.

🔺 A confident dog has a soft expression in the eyes, a relaxed mouth and a tail that swishes from side to side.

Tail

Dogs use their tails to communicate as well as for balance. A wagging tail is hard to interpret correctly as it can indicate anticipation, friendly alertness, caution or extreme tension. Observe the position as well as the speed of the wagging: a high, stiff tail indicates alertness or possible aggression; tucked under and your dog is uncertain or even fearful. When he is relaxed, it will gently swish from side to side.

Multiple signals

Look at all your dog's body language signals and never judge by just the tail movement alone. If he wags his tail while snarling with his ears pinned back, he is unhappy and needs you to give him space and more foundation training to relax him. However, if his ears are softly back and his mouth is relaxed and open while his tail is wagging, he probably wants you to play or stroke him.

What to look for

Confident and relaxed – alert expression, soft eye gaze, ears in mid-position, gentle eye contact.

Happy – same signs as for confident but tail swishing from side to side in mid carriage, corners of mouth pulled back, body upright and back end wagging.

Playful – bright eyes and mouth open; 'play-bow' where bottom is raised into air with front legs lowered, gentle panting.

Stressed (mild) – whites of eyes showing, head lowered or turned away, licking lips or yawning.

Stressed (moderate) – as per mild stress but dog may turn whole body away, tail tucked under, may 'grovel' or roll onto back.

Stressed (extreme) – as mild and medium stress but fixed stare, dilated pupils, lowered head, possibly one front paw raised. If tail upright or stiff arch over back, likely to snap or bite.

Skill 2: Communication

The skill of communicating with your dog is one you need to develop, as it does not come naturally to most humans. Misunderstandings can lead to problems between owners and their dogs, and you will avoid these if you know what your dog is 'saying'. You can learn to read his expressions and body movements through careful observation and assessment; he will be observing your every sound, gesture and intention, too. You should never underestimate how powerful this non-verbal skill can be.

Prediction is key

As you are the person your dog looks to and trusts, many exchanges are based on mutual predictions of each other's behaviour. Your skill will come from looking ahead to what might be about to happen, and acting early so you can intervene. Prediction and early reaction are often seen in professional dog handlers who have a complex working bond with their dog. This skill enables them to articulate what they want intelligently, effectively, and well in advance – you can learn to do this, too.

⬇ Even your scent on a piece of clothing, such as a sock, will carry important messages to your dog.

Your dog is watching you!

You may think you keep a watchful eye on your dog, but he is observing you, too. Even if he is sleeping, he will rouse himself at the first sign of movement or sound. Ask yourself what he is learning from you at all times, not just when you are trying to train him or interact. You may only pay attention to him when he is doing something you don't want him to do, but it would be better to notice and reward him when he is quiet and calm. He will be more likely to repeat the behaviour if it will get your attention.

Scent – the missing skill

You will never be able to replicate your dog's ability to hunt or recognize scent. A dog has a built-in sensor but we need complex equipment to trace scent. Improving scent awareness helps build a more effective partnership with our dogs. If you have just used deodorant or hand wash, it may impact on your dog and will smell very strong indeed to him, possibly interfering with normal communication because he will receive mixed scent information. Likewise, he may indicate that he has found an interesting smell even though you are not aware of it. Learn his scenting body signals: head down for ground scent, head up for air scent, and a look of concentration with his mouth and nose rapidly taking in air.

A dog's eye view

Your dog learns about humans from a lower perspective, bringing children into his eye line. This can be unnerving if he is unaccustomed to this level of contact. Good communication is achieved through mutual recognition of signals, but yours will look very different to your dog than how they appear to you in a mirror. Crouch down and look up at someone giving hand signals, or take a look at your home. You will notice hazards more easily and recognize what are potentially confusing factors for a dog. For example, he may look up at you against the light, seeing your body shape as a silhouette and masking any finer body signals that you are giving.

🔺 **Your dog will see things quite differently from his level and he may even perceive passing traffic as threatening or frightening.**

🔻 **Gentle eye contact allows both the owner and the dog to read each other's body language effectively.**

SKILL
LEVEL

Talk dog

Communication is a two-way process. Your body signals, voice, deliberate and accidental gestures, and even your scent will all combine to deliver complex messages to your dog. To teach and train him effectively, you need to develop the skill of good handling by making sure that you always deliver a consistent and clear message without any confusion. Your dog will be reading you, so self-awareness is key – think about what you are really telling your dog.

Training and communication

Communication means giving and receiving information. Training your dog involves intentional communication from you with a desired outcome from him. Thinking about it in this way means that you can start to give clear signals, or 'cues', to get him to behave in desirable ways. The signals that you employ can be facial expressions, sounds you make with your voice (vocalizations), hand signals and larger body movements. A useful exercise is to watch yourself in the mirror to see what body signals you give. Your dog is probably relying on these for communication more than you realize.

Verbal commands

The average trained dog has been shown to understand around 160 words. In studies, one Border Collie could even recognize objects by name around 70 per cent of the time, an ability that researchers mapped as equivalent to that of a three-year-old child. Nevertheless, humans rely on verbal contact far more than canines. To illustrate this, note the number of vocalizations your dog gives, compared to the human members of your family.

We want our dogs to understand our verbal commands but this is not the canine's first choice for contact. Teach your dog to understand the difference between a verbal command and general daily chatter. Consistency is important, too, and you should train yourself to give clear verbal commands that always sound the same, and make sure other members of the family use the same ones.

Body signals

Your dog reads every part of your body, so bending towards him is perceived as a different signal to standing with your back straight. The movements you make with your feet, such as walking towards him, will often have the effect of slowing him down when he is running towards you.

⬭ Our dogs watch us all the time irrespective of whether our movements are meaningful to them.

⬭ Working dogs, like this intelligent Border Collie, are both exceptional observers and communicators.

Tone of voice

Your dog will learn to recognize the different tones of voice you use for urgency or excitement even when he does not understand the actual words you are saying. He will also be able to understand other people giving the same voice commands, which is indicative of his incredible versatility.

Hand signals

Hand signals develop from food or other rewards, such as toys, used in the hand as a lure. If you have something in your hand that your dog desires, move it around – his eyes, head and body will follow this movement. If you then give him the reward, he will remember this as a positive outcome to his reaction. At first, he will pay attention to your hand because he anticipates that it conceals the reward, but eventually it is the movement of your hand that he notices and follows, regardless of whether the reward is present. The hand signal alone becomes the cue for him to respond. By coupling your hand signals with verbal commands, you can reinforce this message and help your dog comprehend what to do.

Extended signals

Trainers in dog sports, such as 'Heelwork to Music' and trick training, often use a 'target stick' to extend the body signal. This helps the dog to perform more complicated movements. By teaching him to follow the movement of the end of the stick, he learns to attend to this. If you have limited mobility, a target stick may help you to move your dog around more freely.

How your dog learns

Basic learning is the process that leads to relatively permanent changes in your dog's behaviour. As he learns, he alters the way he perceives not only his environment but also how he interprets incoming stimuli, changing the way he behaves or interacts. His behaviour and learning can be affected by external influences as well as by how he feels. Your skill will be to assess what your dog has learned and whether it has been affected by external or internal factors.

⚠ **A dog that feels unwell may hide under a bed to reflect how he feels or he may go there to escape if he is being chased.**

Learning behaviours

Your dog will repeat the actions he finds rewarding but not ones that do not bring rewards. The bigger or more important the reward, the more likely he will be to learn quickly. Equally, the more unpleasant the result, the faster he will learn to avoid that situation again. This is why it is so important to guide your dog's learning to prevent him developing unwanted behaviour.

Rewards

A reward for your dog can be anything he enjoys: a treat, playing with toys, having your attention, meeting and playing with other dogs, or even sleeping. If you know what he wants and what he perceives as a reward at that moment, training him will be easier and more enjoyable. Rewards can be external, such as food, toys, playing games with you, getting your attention or access to other things, including freedom or other dogs. An internal reward is derived from activities that bring on an internal adrenaline rush, such as chasing prey. These can be addictive, encouraging your dog to repeat the behaviour.

Timing is crucial

Reward your dog immediately he does what you ask. He will link certain behaviours to the reward on offer and the command or cue you give. If these are not presented simultaneously, he may not form an association between them all. For example, if you ask your dog to sit and he does so but you do not reward him until he is standing again, he will learn that 'sit' actually means 'stand up'.

Behaviour 'chains'

Dogs are expert at forming links between events and outcomes, sometimes predicting possible results well in advance. Your dog can link the time of day with you picking up your coat or even looking out of the window as a sign that he may be going for a walk long before you say anything or hold his lead. He has learned a chain of behaviours, and understanding these will form a fundamental part of your training practice.

Aversion training

The idea that a dog is deserving of punishment when he makes a mistake is outmoded and unfair. Build a bond of trust with your dog. Don't be afraid to interrupt him when he does something wrong; instead, divert him quickly to a more suitable action. Punishment is usually ill-timed, making him feel that you, or people or dogs around him, are associated with it and he will become nervous and defensive. Don't use harsh or forceful methods, such as yanking his lead or forcing him into situations he would rather avoid; this is damaging and potentially dangerous if he bites through fear or pain.

🔺 Try not to allow your dog to steal food as it is a self-rewarding behaviour that can be really hard to eradicate.

🔺 You can reward good behaviour with an edible chew or treat.

SKILL
LEVEL

Different breeds

Dogs are all one species even though specific breeds look different and exhibit a wide range of behaviours. They have been deliberately bred to enhance their qualities over centuries of association with humans. Your choice of breed should be based on your needs and lifestyle rather than physical appearance to ensure a more satisfying relationship between you and your dog.

Terriers

With their fast-reactions and a tendency to work alone, terriers are hardy and independent with strong and determined characters. Training is essential for developing a strong bond with your terrier as well as teaching him that he must look to you for decisions before he reacts. Terriers can be highly vocal and make good watchdogs.

Herding or livestock guardian dogs

These dogs, which include Border Collies and German Shepherds, evolved to work alongside their human companions, protecting livestock or property. Incredibly sensitive, they have lots of energy and are also easily motivated in training. However, their powerful working intelligence can make them challenging to own.

Bull terriers

These powerful dogs are unfairly maligned. Often good with people but with a powerful chase and play instinct with other dogs, they can become over-stimulated. You must always control your Bull Terrier in public and have a very strict set of rules about strength games, such as tugging and snatching.

Gundogs

Highly effective at working with their owners to retrieve game, dogs such as Retrievers and Spaniels can make energetic pets. You must have enough space and time for these breeds as they need plenty of stimulation. Motivate and train your gundog with games and retrieve exercises.

Crossbreeds

Never assume that a crossbreed is automatically healthier than a pedigree; make sure you check the health and temperament of both parents before selecting one. You may get the best of both breeds or their more difficult aspects. However, that said, most crossbred dogs are a delight to own.

Hounds

Sight hounds, such as Greyhounds, have excellent vision at long distances and are very athletic, reaching great speeds when chasing prey. They are often laid back when they're not being stimulated by movement. Scent hounds have excellent noses and can air or ground scent easily. Hounds have been bred to hunt in packs but can still be quite independent, so you may have to work hard to teach your dog to follow your lead in training.

Toy dogs

Chihuahuas, Papillons and Pugs are bred to be small and enjoy human company and comfort but can be just as strong-willed as bigger breeds. They are often motivated by attention and need to learn how to deal with constant approaches from people and to enjoy being picked up as well as not being afraid to walk in busy, crowded places.

Giant breeds

Many giant breeds were bred for jobs that take advantage of their size: pulling carts and guard dogs. It takes hard work and time to maintain their health and physical condition – and they are expensive to feed. These dogs need careful training from an early age to ensure they do not take advantage of their size by pulling you around.

Ownership and leadership

SKILL
LEVEL

Your dog has not learned the rules of the human world and therefore he needs your guidance and leadership. Even though our dogs, as a species, have been around for as long as humans, they do not understand the minutiae of modern life, such as good manners, road safety and laws about aggressive dogs.

⬆ **A stairgate provides a physical boundary that allows for control and safety management.**

Your role

Your duty as an owner is to be a leader or guardian, keeping your dog safe and teaching him how to act in the human world. You are legally responsible for his behaviour, but you should never assume that he realizes this. Always make sure that you keep your dog securely on a lead by the roadside, train him to have a rock-solid recall and never allow bad habits or nervousness to build up and become a problem.

Setting boundaries

Set – and insist upon – firm boundaries of acceptable behaviour for your dog to learn and follow. You can allow him onto the sofa or chairs if you wish, but he must get down when asked. Never feed him at meal times when you are seated at the table if you don't want him to beg constantly afterwards. Nor should you allow a puppy to move forward on a tight lead if you don't want him to become an adult dog that pulls you on walks. Other boundaries are physical, such as a stairgate to prevent your dog going upstairs or into certain rooms. Try using a houseline, which is a slightly longer version of a lead, to teach him to move from place to place if he refuses to follow your commands.

Controlling resources

As the guardian of your dog, you must have complete control over all potential rewards. Resources in the form of food and toys are the most tangible ones, but attention, touch, visitors and freedom are all powerful and valuable rewards for your dog. These are all part of your daily negotiations for training and instilling good behaviour. For instance, if you don't want your dog to dash out of the door, withhold the resource of freedom until he sits and waits whilst the door is opened – do not let him move until you step through. To stop him jumping up at visitors, ensure that he is not allowed to greet or be greeted until he is calm; put a lead on him if necessary to prevent him moving. Visitors can be a valuable and exciting reward, so make him work for this.

Your dog's place in his human family

Most canine experts no longer believe that dogs are submissive or dominant within a rigid hierarchical structure. Instead, research has shown that they form individual relationships with fellow dogs and members of their human family. You may have more control over your dog than other people in your family, or you may find that he is more obedient for them than for you. If you learn his individual likes, dislikes and priorities, he is more likely to behave well for you. For example, he may not be very interested in treats or playing with toys but may love your attention and companionship and when you touch his ears. If this is the case, use this as a touch reward every time you wish to praise him.

▲ **Controlling your dog in public places is part of your role in the dog-owner team.**

▲ **All training is teamwork, and it should be fun. You can reward your dog's good behaviour with a game.**

Teamwork

Your dog may make some decisions that could be potentially harmful. This is not deliberately 'naughty'. You are his trainer, helper, companion and carer, so help him to stay out of troublesome situations. If you anticipate problems, you can prevent them happening and help him to cope. All dog training is teamwork, never simply a case of 'bad owners' or 'bad dogs'.

SKILL
LEVEL

Basic training: Sit!

Begin your training in a quiet place with no distractions. Make sure that you have some tasty, soft and smelly food to hand, such as tiny pieces of cheese or chicken. This avoids overfeeding and enables you to offer several treats in one go to reward success if your dog is doing really well. Always keep all your training sessions short, no more than five minutes at a stretch. It's better to fit several into each day rather than focus on one long session.

Teach your dog to sit

The sit command is fundamental. It acts as a perfect anchor to stop your dog jumping up or chasing, and keeps him steady when there are distractions.

▶ **1** Hold a small food treat in your hand and show it to your dog. Move your hand to get him interested in the food.

▶ **2** Use your hand as a lure, keeping it on his nose, and then raise it slightly until his head lifts. Move it over his head, towards the back of his neck. As he follows your hand, his bottom should lower to the ground to enable him to reach the food. He will end up in a sitting position.

⬆ **3** As soon as his bottom touches the ground, give the command 'Sit', praise him and release the treat while he is still seated. Repeat the exercise several times until he begins to anticipate what you want.

Take it further

- Start saying 'Sit' just before you start moving your hand. Use a clearly visible hand signal with your hand lifted slightly upwards.
- Practise until you can say the word and lift your hand slightly to get him to sit without him having to follow your hand so closely. Praise him each time he does it before you release the treat.
- Start using a 'release' command, such as 'Off you go', when it is time for him to move off the spot.

Troubleshooting

If he snatches the food
Keep the treats small and frequent, so he does not become frustrated. If he is very food-motivated and gets highly over-excited at the food you are using, try something less interesting.

If he jumps at the food
Your hand is too high above his head. Lower it to his nose to allow him to sniff and follow your hand.

If he shows no interest
Use tastier food in a place with fewer distractions or consider that he may be tired or over stimulated – or simply not hungry!

If he moves too early
Move him back to the same spot and start again. Don't bend over him. It may help if you train him to sit at your side instead of in front of you. Stay upright and move naturally and confidently, but don't take your eyes off him. If you are not looking at him, you won't spot the early signs that he is about to make a mistake or be able to help him avoid this.

SKILL
LEVEL

Basic training: Come!

Always perform this training exercise in a calm environment, armed with some tasty food treats and a favourite toy that squeaks or can be moved about, so your dog can see it easily. A ball or 'ragger' toy is ideal, and it fits comfortably into your pocket when you're out walking with your dog.

Teach your dog to come

1 With your dog nearby, suddenly produce a treat or toy and call him excitedly by name. Crouch down with your arms invitingly open and keep your facial expression happy.

2 Show your dog the food or the toy, moving it around to get him really interested, and then call him to you, using the command 'Come!'.

3 As soon as he comes, make a fuss of him and give him his treat and reward him with a game. Repeat several times, so he learns that it's worth coming to you as you have something of great value: your attention and praise, his treat and his toy.

Take it further

- When you're out walking with your dog on the lead, suddenly dash away from him and say the command 'Come!'. Use the lead to gently encourage him to follow you but try to attract him with welcoming, crouching body language and his treat or toy reward.
- When he reliably turns towards you on your command, you can give him more freedom. Practise calling him back to you regularly, always making it an exciting game.
- Gradually add more distractions to this exercise, such as other people or dogs at a distance, and anticipate your dog's likely reactions, so you can prevent situations in which he may become too distracted to listen to you. Continue to build up a reliable, rock-solid recall.

A long line helps maintain control during the training process and reinforces your commands simply and effectively.

Troubleshooting

If he grabs the reward and runs away
Take hold of his collar just before you release any rewards. This will give him confidence in the hand reaching towards him and he will not attempt to dodge out of the way. He will anticipate the reward instead.

If he runs off to other dogs and people
You have probably not built up your training steadily enough; some dogs are highly motivated by social contact with others and need extra help. Put him on a long trailing line and keep a close eye on him. If he ignores your command, use the line to reel him in. This confirms that he must obey your instruction.

If he dodges past
It is possible that he fears your reaction or you are bending forwards, which can look playful or even threatening to a dog. Stand up straight or crouch with your back straight. Use a long line to guide him back to you and ensure that the reward is really enjoyable.

SKILL
LEVEL

Basic training: walking to heel

If your dog has a tendency to pull on the lead, it can lead to a breakdown in the bond between you. Most dogs respond to a tight lead by pulling even harder, so keep the lead loose and learn to relax – you can transmit tense body language to your dog. If he wants to move forward, it has to be on your terms. Note that this exercise does not rely on food or toy rewards.

Teach your dog to walk at your side

1 Start by encouraging your dog to trot happily at your side on a loose lead.

2 He must learn to follow your feet when they move and to stop when they stop. When he is at your side and the lead is loose, praise him if he walks at the same time as your own feet.

Choke chains

Avoid any devices that rely on physical correction, such as choke chains. These damage your dog's trachea and spine and can cause eye problems. They rely on causing pain to teach him not to pull. It is easier to teach your dog to walk beside you than to punish him for getting it wrong.

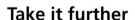 **3** If he forges ahead, stop immediately, and then take one or two steps backwards while, simultaneously, steering him round and back towards your side.

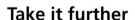 **4** Bring him back to your side, wait a few seconds, relax the lead, and then begin again. He will soon learn that if the lead goes taut, he will not only stop moving but will also end up further back than when he started.

Note: Walk normally and naturally and always be prepared to stop and re-position your dog when he goes wrong. At first this may happen every few paces, but when he realizes that there is no tension on his neck, he won't want to lunge forwards to overcome that sensation.

Take it further

- Practise walking your dog with ever more tempting distractions and in busy environments; always insist that he stays next to you with the lead loose.
- When he is walking reliably next to your side on a loose lead, say the 'Heel' command. When he associates this command with that position, you can use this verbal cue to guide him into your side.

Troubleshooting

If he rears up
Position your hands low and your elbows at your sides as you take a pace backwards. This will keep all of his four feet firmly on the ground.

If he is hard to manage
Invest in some training aids to control his strength. Front-connecting, no-pull harnesses and head-collars are gentle and effective ways of establishing physical control. They can provide extra safety if you have reduced mobility or your dog is fast-reacting and may lunge and pull you over.

Skill 3: Understanding

Your dog has many needs and, as an understanding owner, it is your duty to satisfy them. Your responsibilities include providing him with companionship and a safe and secure environment, feeding him a healthy diet, and fulfilling his health and general welfare requirements, such as allowing him to behave naturally. To develop this skill you must familiarize yourself with all these categories and regularly review his health. His needs may vary from those of your previous dogs, so take care to treat him as an individual.

Health issues

- Some breeds can be prone to eye health problems caused by drooping lids or protrusion of the third eyelid. This is more common in flat-faced (brachycephalic) dogs with prominent eyes, such as Pugs, as well as Basset Hounds and some giant breeds (Great Danes).

- Maintaining good dental health through regular mouth examination and teeth cleaning can prevent tartar building up and causing infection. Get your dog used to having his mouth checked to prevent him becoming fearful of human touch.

Choose a healthy dog

A healthy and happy dog will give you maximum enjoyment, so health considerations are a priority when you are choosing your future companion.

Good genes
Myriad genetic conditions can afflict different breeds, and interbreeding can accentuate features to the point where a dog's quality of life is severely affected. By doing your research carefully and choosing wisely – important factors that are often overlooked in favour of fashion or appearances – you and your dog are more likely to have a successful and happy life together.

Early nurturing necessities
Try to ensure that your new dog has good behavioural as well as physical health. Before you take your puppy home at around eight weeks, see both his parents in order to assess his temperament. If you are taking on a rescue dog, get as much information as possible about him and his background from the staff at the rescue centre. Early experiences for any dog are significant factors in future successful ownership. If your puppy has been reared in a busy household and exposed to a range of people, animals, electrical appliances and other experiences, he will have already learned an essential life skill that no amount of training can replace in later life.

Physical health

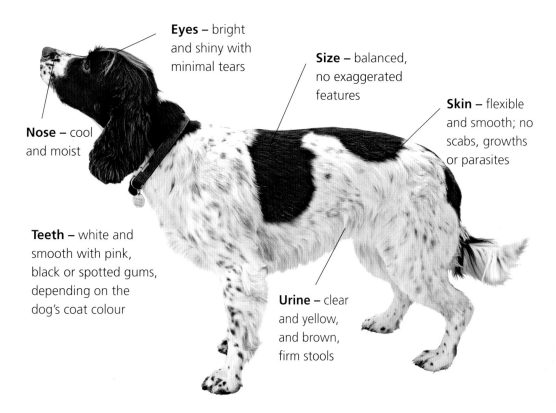

Eyes – bright and shiny with minimal tears

Size – balanced, no exaggerated features

Skin – flexible and smooth; no scabs, growths or parasites

Nose – cool and moist

Teeth – white and smooth with pink, black or spotted gums, depending on the dog's coat colour

Urine – clear and yellow, and brown, firm stools

🔺 **Regular examination of your dog's teeth helps to prevent extensive dental treatment later in life.**

Signs of behavioural health

- **Posture** – confident but relaxed.
- **Expression** – alert but soft.
- **Mouth** – soft with corners drawn up.
- **Ears** – in 'neutral' position.
- **Paws and flanks** – no chewing or hair loss.

Obesity

Although it is not a disease in itself, obesity is related to many health conditions and is increasingly common in dogs. Make sure that your dog gets adequate exercise and a balanced, good-quality diet.

Recognizing signs of ill health

SKILL LEVEL

Your dog's physical and behavioural health are closely interlinked but he does not display symptoms of illness or pain in the same way as you. It is important to learn to read the early signs, such as reluctance or over-enthusiasm to eat or drink, frequent toileting, or agitated activity (scratching or chewing at his paws). Identifying stress signals (see page 19) can also be helpful. An elderly dog, or one that is in pain, may simply slow down or no longer jump up onto his favourite chair. Some dogs may avoid their owners or even growl or exhibit aggressive behaviour, which is totally unexpected and out of character. You should always contact your vet at the first signs of ill health.

🔺 Keep a regular check on your dog's health, looking for any signs of lameness.

What to look for

Get to know your dog's habits: the skill of maintaining good health is to look for uncharacteristic behaviours. A previously laid-back dog may suddenly show signs of hyperactivity, whereas a highly active dog may prefer to stay in his bed. More obvious signs, such as sores, cuts, lumps and swellings, are easier to spot, but never assume that all illnesses or behaviour problems manifest themselves so clearly. Familiarize yourself with breed-specific problems, such as hip dysplasia in German Shepherd Dogs, Golden and Labrador Retrievers, and Great Danes. If your dog is lame or is experiencing difficulty climbing steps, consult your vet who may recommend an X-ray to help with diagnosis.

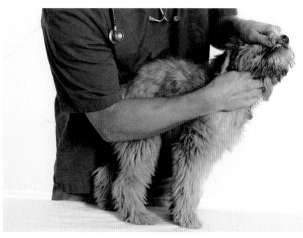

▶ Visit your vet if you have any health concerns – dogs do not readily show pain.

Regular health checks

Perform a daily health check on your dog as part of your grooming or play routine – he will enjoy your touch and close handling. He does not have to stand up to be examined – a belly rub will allow you to feel his anatomy just as closely. Check his eyes, ears, mouth and teeth, and examine his coat carefully for any fleas and ticks, especially in summer. Make sure that he is urinating and defecating normally. Some minor health problems may not require veterinary treatment, but if you feel he is unwell always contact your local veterinary practice to describe his symptoms and ask for their advice.

Mental and behavioural signs

Your dog will benefit from your companionship, mental exercise and a regular routine to help him maintain good behavioural health. If left unaddressed, behaviour problems usually worsen, so they should be dealt with as soon as they appear. If necessary seek professional help from an accredited pet behaviour counsellor.

⬥ **Grass seeds can easily work their way from your dog's coat to his skin, causing infection. Always check him over after exercise and consult your vet if necessary.**

Is my dog unwell?

Bad breath – may be a sign of periodontal disease (infection of the gums and surrounding tissues), tartar build-up, or a mouth infection. It occurs in 85 per cent of dogs over the age of three unless you provide regular dental homecare.

Eyes – inflamed or cloudy eyes may be a sign of ulceration, conjunctivitis or glaucoma. See your vet at the first sign of problems.

Ear problems – these are painful and distressing, and your dog may react badly to being petted, shake his head frantically and exhibit balance problems. They can be due to infection or a foreign body, e.g. grass seed.

Skin problems – if your dog is scratching or has hair loss, check for parasites or sores. They can be signs of stress.

Stomach swelling – can be a sign of torsion or 'bloat' and is an emergency. The dog becomes breathless and very distressed.

Digestion – loose stools or blood/mucus can signal digestive problems. Vomiting can be caused by a blockage, worms or poisoning.

SKILL
LEVEL

Preventing health problems

You can help to prevent health problems by examining your dog regularly, controlling parasites and checking his behaviour. Use tasty treats to encourage and reassure him, and he will enjoy this special time together. Get him used to this on a daily basis, so he won't mind you inspecting him if he's unwell.

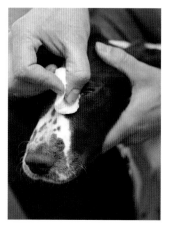

⚠ **Good eye hygiene is essential and helps prevent tear staining.**

⚠ **Regular vaccinations can prevent serious disease.**

Vaccinations

You can protect your dog from serious diseases, such as distemper, leptospirosis, parvovirus and kennel cough, by getting him vaccinated. He will need his first course of injections when he's a puppy. Your vet will advise how frequently he needs to be immunized throughout his life. If you plan to travel abroad with him, he will need further and additional vaccinations and preventative medical treatment; ask your vet what is appropriate.

Worms

Worms are common and may not be apparent in your dog unless they are present in large numbers. New types are beginning to appear, possibly as a result of climate change, and they can live in the organs or major blood vessels and cause severe illness or even death. Familiarize yourself with the potential signs, usually an upset tummy and 'scooting' along the floor, and ensure you worm your dog regularly and never allow him to eat litter or animal faeces. Puppies are particularly at risk; they may pick up worms from their mother and need worming at an early age. Worms can also be passed on through flea infestation or, in some countries, by mosquito bites.

Health and genetic screening

Canine health schemes can screen for many inherited conditions and reduce the incidence of genetic diseases in specific breeds. Do your research before choosing a dog to make sure the breeder has done the relevant genetic screening checks before you agree to buy a puppy. Inherited conditions, such as hip dysplasia, elbow dysplasia and many eye diseases, can all be tested for.

Find out if there are any specialist courses teaching first aid skills for pet owners in your area. You will learn how to deal with a wide range of minor problems as well as the best course of action in an emergency.

Fleas and ticks

Our modern centrally heated homes provide the ideal environment for fleas to breed all year round. They survive by ingesting blood through a dog's skin several times a day. The telltale signs are small sooty specks in your dog's coat. Brush him and allow some of them to fall onto a damp white tissue – they will leave a red mark. Your vet will advise you on the most suitable treatments and preventative measures. These are usually applied painlessly as a small amount of solution between your dog's shoulder blades. Make sure you treat his home environment, too – vacuum all his bedding and the sofa cushions regularly as well as focusing on carpets and floors.

Ticks often attach themselves to a dog's head, and they look similar to warts. If your dog likes to roam in long grass or woodland, he may become infested, so check him over regularly. Ask your vet to show you how to remove ticks safely.

DNA screening

DNA is a record of a dog's genetic profile. It can be used to identify dogs that may be clear from, a carrier of, or affected by a medical condition. It helps responsible breeders to assess the likelihood of puppies developing genetic conditions. Investigate your chosen breed's potential problems and check whether the litters you plan to view have been DNA screened.

Puppies and their parents can be screened, and the results should be openly declared either by the breeder or on the breed register. Ask to see them before deciding to purchase a dog. You can also get information about your chosen breed's genetic health by asking your vet or breeder to recommend resources. Do your research.

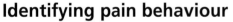

Mental and behavioural health

SKILL
LEVEL

Many behaviour-related difficulties are linked to physical or medical problems, so before seeking an accredited behaviourist, get your dog examined by a vet. If he is acting out of character or developing unwanted traits, don't suffer in silence – seek help. Some unwanted behaviours can only be improved with a thorough behaviour assessment and modification programme.

Acting early

If you are familiar with how your dog likes to play and interact, you will be able to intervene as soon as a problem arises. For example, if he starts following you around the house and appears worried when you leave, prevent further anxiety by gradually 'detaching' yourself on an everyday basis, so he learns to cope with being left alone. Never hope that behaviour problems will go away by themselves – you must help to solve them by making the necessary changes to his environment.

Identifying pain behaviour

Some behavioural health problems manifest themselves as a result of pain, so you must investigate this possibility. Your dog may show that he is in pain through a change in his demeanour and responses to people and other dogs, by altered posture, limited mobility and reduced activity. He may yelp or whimper or simply avoid being touched, particularly in the painful area. When assessing

▲ Your dog must learn to stay calm and relaxed when he is left alone at home.

◀ Separation anxiety is a common behaviour problem causing stress, house soiling and destruction. If your dog is affected, maybe you should consider seeking expert assistance.

him, keep him quiet and comfortable; if he is in pain there's a higher risk of him reacting aggressively. If he has an accident, always ask your vet to check him over.

Breed and behaviour

Different breeds vary in their needs for maintaining behavioural health. Border Collies require a great deal of stimulation and exercise or they may get stressed and frustrated, leading to hyperactivity, destructive behaviour and even aggression. Labradors and Retrievers often enjoy holding things in their mouths and need an outlet for this in toys or retrieving games. If these are not provided they can develop behaviour problems, including possessiveness or stealing, sometimes leading to ingesting unsuitable items, such as pebbles or clothing. Pastoral breeds, like German Shepherd Dogs, were bred to protect livestock or property and can manifest these 'natural' behaviours in the home, which can pose a risk to visitors. Terriers, which were developed to keep down vermin, can sometimes use their instincts by chasing cats. Review your dog's needs to assess what he enjoys and learn to direct these instincts in a suitable way.

Difficult to read?

Some breeds can be difficult to read through physical signs as their expressions and body language are hard to read and they do not give you many clues. These include Mastiffs and dogs with strong physical characteristics, such as the Shar Pei. Again, getting to know your own dog and becoming an expert on his moods is the key to successful maintenance of behavioural health.

🔻 **Give active dogs ways to express their hunting and retrieving instincts.**

SKILL
LEVEL

Common behaviour problems

Learn to recognize the early symptoms of problem behaviours long before they develop into major ones. They can be hard to eradicate because they involve a learning process that cannot be easily unlearned. Once a bad habit is established, you must replace it with a preferred one. Your dog will have to choose between them and can easily revert back to the unwanted behaviour, a process known as spontaneous recovery. If you do not stop him jumping up at visitors as a friendly puppy he will learn that this is normal behaviour and will do it when he is a large adult. Teach him to sit instead, although he will not forget the enjoyment of this greeting behaviour and could easily revert.

⬆ **Jumping up to greet people can be easily controlled by teaching your dog an alternative behaviour, such as sitting.**

Frustration

Frustration can cause a range of behaviour problems, including barking at other dogs and pulling on the lead. Young dogs do not cope well with delayed rewards and can often grab in an effort to reach items they would like. With carefully paced training you can teach your dog to control his impulses to snatch and lunge. This helps him to understand that rewards are given as part of the learning process. If he feels he cannot achieve what is on offer he may become frustrated, so always keep your training sessions short and make sure he finishes on a success. Allow him to play with other dogs as a reward for staying calm. Teach him that pulling on the lead does not bring him closer to target people or places, but walking on a loose lead will be rewarded.

Separation

Dogs are companion animals and thrive on social contact. Your dog must learn from an early age to cope with being left alone as well as enjoying time with you. Many behaviour problems are linked to dogs being left at home alone and they can take a long time to solve. In your role as guardian, you must ensure that your dog does not suffer in this way. Isolation distress is when a dog does not like being alone, whereas separation distress occurs when he may be hyper-attached to his owner. In each case, make sure your dog has additional rewards when

⬆ **Loose lead training helps your dog to control his impulses and makes walks more enjoyable for both of you.**

you are separated to replace the important companion who is not present. Long-lasting toys he can investigate and enjoy, perhaps containing cheese spread or peanut butter, can help to alleviate and prevent distress.

Possessive behaviour

If your dog places a high value on food items or toys this can lead to possessive behaviour. You may notice that he stiffens and stares when someone is near while he is eating or playing. Teach him that food and toys are plentiful and there is no reason to protect or defend them. Swap items you do not wish him to have for high-value treats, such as small pieces of cheese, ham or chicken, or perhaps a more tempting toy. Simply taking items, such as a food bowl, away from your dog teaches him to be extremely possessive and does not put you in charge. He will only learn to defend them more vigorously next time. Resources should be based on negotiation principles to enable your dog to understand how to achieve them. You must show him that you control resources by allowing him to have these in return for acceptable behaviour, such as sitting patiently and quietly or coming back to you on a walk.

Destructive dogs

Puppies destroy items through exploratory play, but boredom and anxiety can also lead to destructive behaviour. Protect valuable items, and give your dog plenty to do whilst he is alone, using safe chew toys and treat balls in which you have placed a portion of his dinner. If you want to use a puppy pen or crate to keep him safe and contained within a small area, be sure to introduce it very gradually as your dog might easily feel trapped and may even panic. A crate must only ever be used for short periods. Consider employing a dog walker to visit if you have to go out for longer periods.

⬆ **Access to windows can lead to guarding problems.**

SKILL 4: MOTIVATION

Skill 4: Motivation

SKILL LEVEL

A healthy, happy dog needs a balance of good diet and plenty of exercise outlets for his energy through a mixture of games and playing with you and other dogs as well as basic hygiene and health care requirements, such as staying clean and well-groomed. It's your job to provide these for your dog.

Sanctuary

Bonding with your dog means you rely on him for comfort and enjoyment while providing safety and reassurance. A fearful dog is often allowed to make his own decisions under pressure, and only relaxes when his owner takes control. Provide a guiding hand: never physically punish him – show him better, preferred options. Train him to focus on you at times of potential stress by giving him a simple task, such as a sit.

Satisfying needs

Dogs vary in their needs: terriers and Collies can be highly reactive and need careful socializing, while Labradors are people-dependent and do not cope well with separation. Your dog relies on you to act responsibly and care for him in ways that meet his needs while working within our human boundaries. This is very important for all dogs but especially so for larger and more powerful breeds that have attracted adverse publicity in recent times.

Keeping your dog safe

Your dog relies on you to keep him safe, secure and protected from the everyday hazards in the world around him. He will not realize the dangers that surround modern living, ranging from traffic safety to chewing on electric cables, and you must take care of this by providing a safe environment inside and outside your home.

◀ Regular walks with friends help to exercise your dog and give you motivation, too.

46

Safeguards

Your dog must wear a visible identification tag with your name, address and telephone numbers inscribed on it. A small dog may need a double-sided tag, or even two disks, to display the information. Visible ID means that anyone can identify and return him if he goes missing. You should also ensure that he is microchipped; this simple procedure only takes seconds to carry out and will identify your dog in a national data base when scanned.

Shelter

Your dog needs to sleep in a warm, clean, dry and draught-free place, preferably indoors. Keeping him outdoors can lead to behaviour problems, such as barking and fence-guarding, particularly if he has free-roaming access. Dogs hear and react to external noises and respond by barking an alert signal, which can disturb neighbours. Your dog may patrol boundaries and develop a territorial attitude towards your property; if this habit becomes ingrained he may not welcome visitors to your home, even friends and family members.

Surveillance

You should always know where your dog is at any given time. In public he must be under your control, especially off lead, since other dogs and people can easily attract his attention. Develop a habit of scanning the horizon, and don't forget to check behind you as well, when your dog is loose.

🔺 Alert and active dogs need regular stimulation to avoid behaviour problems.

◀ Your dog needs to wear some form of visible identification to comply with legal requirements.

Exercise and rest

SKILL LEVEL

Achieving a good balance between exercise and rest will keep your dog fit, healthy and lean. He will be more tired and less likely to misbehave. Most adult dogs need around 30–60 minutes of exercise per day or more, depending on their physical size as well as the work they have been bred to perform.

High-energy dogs

Working breeds, such as Labrador Retrievers, Border Collies and German Shepherds, often have a huge amount of energy and can be destructive if not given an outlet. Walking your high-energy dog will not be enough to occupy his active mind, and he will need fun games and interesting training to make sure his unspent enthusiasm does not become a problem. While he is young, provide a variety of safe items for him to chew, such as hollow rubber toys containing small amounts of tasty food. Chewing can be calming and helps save chair legs, walls and doors from damage.

⬆ **Powerful retrieve instincts in some breeds need a suitable outlet, such as playing with toys.**

Small dogs

Small breeds, like Chihuahuas and Cavalier King Charles Spaniels, can be very energetic and will happily play with larger dogs. Your small dog may enjoy curling up on your lap, but he will still want walks and games. Avoid the temptation to carry him everywhere – a dog carrier can

⬇ **Small dogs can be just as energetic as larger ones.**

Swimming

Your dog may enjoy playing in water; you can even buy floating toys for this purpose. However, take precautions and never allow him to swim where he cannot get out of the water easily or there might be a fast-flowing current. Some water is affected by algae and other organisms, some of which may be toxic, so check this with your local environment authority. If your dog has mobility problems, he may enjoy swimming in a hydrotherapy pool.

be useful in situations where he might get trodden on but he must be well socialized and allowed to stand on his own four feet. Teach him that people stroking him are fun and offer him a treat each time to make it a pleasant experience for him. Small dogs attract a lot of attention, especially from children, so make sure he is ready for this.

Interactive exercise

Your dog will benefit from a varied exercise routine, including familiar walks in his local environment where he can catch up on the latest scents. Let him sniff and urine mark out of doors to activate his senses and enrich his experience of what might seem a humdrum walk to you. Take him to a wide range of locations: woods, parks, beaches and town centres. Travel by bus or train to new places. Exercising your dog in this way gives him plenty of messages about his world as well as making him confident about new experiences. Playing with other dogs should also be a regular part of his daily exercise routine. Familiarize yourself with local areas where he can meet and play safely with his canine companions.

Rest

Your dog needs a surprising amount of rest and may sleep between 13 and 18 hours per day. This is usually in shorter naps than we take and varies according to age and breed. If your puppy behaves badly, he may be overtired, so let him rest in a quiet place to wind down.

A healthy diet

SKILL
LEVEL

Healthy dogs need a good-quality, well-balanced diet. Dogs can be classed as carnivorous but they do adapt well to a wide-ranging diet and will eat and digest vegetables and grains as well as meat. They must always have access to a fresh supply of clean water, which must be changed several times daily.

Take care!

Keep all foodstuffs well out of reach along with any smaller items that are easy to pick up or swallow. Stones, children's toys, nails and even mobile phones have been removed surgically from dogs' stomachs. If you notice that your dog has a tendency to pick up non-food items, react calmly and encourage him to bring you the item, then swap it for a food treat. If you panic and shout, he is more likely to run away to protect his prize, or may simply swallow the item.

Food choices

There are so many options for your dog's dinner, from home-cooked or canned food to dry pellets or kibble. There are no set rules governing which food is best, so choose the one that suits your lifestyle and aim for as natural a diet as possible. Take care to look at the ingredients rather than the packaging, which is designed to attract humans to buy the products and does not reflect their nutritional content. Be aware that some foods are age-related: puppy food is formulated to meet the needs of a growing young dog, and there are also specialist products to meet the needs of elderly dogs.

▶ Make healthy choices for your dog's dinner as this can affect his behaviour as well as his physical wellbeing and fitness.

🔺 **Never ever feed dogs of any age from a single bowl as it creates serious food guarding problems.**

▶ **Always monitor your dog's food intake and avoid giving him leftovers.**

Obesity

An obese dog weighs around 20 per cent above his normal body weight and will suffer impaired health, welfare and quality of life as a direct result. If your dog is overweight but otherwise healthy, the food he is eating contains more energy than he is using. Some breeds, such as Labrador Retrievers, are very greedy and have a high risk of obesity, and this increases with age. It is also more common in spayed bitches than male dogs. Obese dogs can suffer from orthopaedic and heart problems along with many other medical conditions that can shorten their lives, including diabetes.

The owners of obese dogs are more likely to be obese than people with fit, slim dogs, so this may reflect general over-eating or lack of exercise in both parties. Try to maintain a balanced diet for your dog, and if, for any reason, you feel he is putting on weight, ask your vet for advice and to rule out any potential illness.

Diet guidelines

- Get into the habit of reading the labels on dog food, so you can measure out the correct amount for your dog's size and weight.

- Do not worry if he is not overly enthusiastic about his regular food unless you notice sudden changes in his weight or if he is underweight.

- Never try to entice him to eat by adding high-calorie additions to his food, as this can make him more demanding as well as overweight and unhealthy.

- Some dogs prefer to graze throughout the day rather than eat one large meal, so adopt a relaxed attitude to your dog's eating habits.

- If your dog normally eats well but suddenly refuses food, seek veterinary advice as he may be ill.

Toxic foods

Some foods you enjoy are toxic for your dog. They include chocolate, onions, grapes, macadamia nuts, raisins and xylitol, an artificial sweetener. Be careful about feeding and treating him.

Games and play

SKILL
LEVEL

These are very important for your dog's wellbeing and you should learn to recognize the 'play-bow' in which he raises his rear end high in the air and lowers the front of his body as he elicits a game. With familiar playmates, this gesture may shorten into a simple 'play slap' whereby he quickly jabs both forepaws onto the ground before dashing off, bouncing, lungeing and play-growling. As well as playing with dogs, humans and other animals, your dog will enjoy indulging in solitary play, especially with favourite toys.

⬤ **Play exercises your dog physically and mentally, as well as being an important and enjoyable part of his regular daily routine.**

Play to learn

Play helps your dog to learn safely about social signals and co-operation with other dogs as well as humans. It involves milder versions or mimicry of instinctive gestures. Play with toys helps to satisfy instincts where the opportunity to hunt for live prey may not be suitable. For a puppy, play is a 'role-playing' rehearsal for real-life interactions, starting with mouthing at three weeks of age. At 16 weeks, he will develop more sophisticated play skills with objects, begin chewing and enjoy chasing.

Play training

You can direct your dog's play in such a way that he learns good manners within acceptable boundaries. Do this by incorporating training exercises, such as a settle down and stay to teach him control over objects and to calm down at times of excitement. Never allow boundaries to become 'blurred': inconsistency causes confusion about the messages you are trying to teach.

Social play

Your dog learns from you about how to interact with people, so never engage in rough, uncontrolled contact. Puppies mouth each other's face and neck, 'jaw wrestle' and roll each other over. If play becomes too vigorous, one pup may yelp or run away. This teaches the other puppy to play more gently next time if the fun is to continue. Insist your dog plays gently with you, so he does not adopt a boisterous play style with other

⬤ **Always encourage your dog to play games with you to help build a strong bond and have fun together.**

Predatory play

Dogs enjoy games that engage their predatory instincts, especially hunting, chasing and carrying. Hide some treats under a set of cups and allow your dog to sniff for them, or play a game of hide and seek so he can search for you. Don't let him chase cats or small animals as this encourages a chase instinct which is difficult to control. Play retrieve games with toys with a controlled end result.

humans, especially the frail, the elderly, young children, visitors and passers-by who may misinterpret this as dangerous or threatening behaviour. Teach your dog to enjoy rough and tumble only at light intensity. If he begins to get over-exuberant, stop playing immediately.

Chewing and mouthing

Your puppy chews as a natural and enjoyable part of his development and this is how he learns about the world. Let him chew only safe, suitable items, such as hollow rubber toys containing a tasty treat. This stops him chewing your furniture, alleviates teething discomfort and helps reduce stress, so he can cope better when left alone. Teach him to develop a regular chewing habit using safe, indestructible toys designed for dogs.

▼ **Simple hunting games not only stimulate your dog mentally but also demonstrate his superior scenting skills.**

Socialization

SKILL
LEVEL

Your dog must develop a healthy familiarity with a range of sights, sounds, people and environments if he is to cope with everyday life. This is known as socialization, and evidence shows that dogs that are not adequately socialized can exhibit a range of behavioural problems. As soon as you bring your new puppy home you must make this a priority. At its most effective, socialization peaks between eight and eleven weeks of age (the 'critical period') but it is an ongoing process and continues throughout your dog's life. Make a chart of the experiences your puppy should have and ensure each area is completed.

Begin at the breeder

Socialization starts in the breeder's home and, ideally, your puppy should begin his life in a household with normal bustle and noise. Puppies become aware of their surroundings gradually as their senses develop – as early as three weeks old. Never buy from a pet shop, kennels or breeder where the puppies are not in constant contact with people. Puppies raised in these conditions are at high risk of fearful behaviour in later life as they struggle to cope with stress and new situations.

Meeting other dogs

Many veterinary practices run puppy play sessions where they can mix safely, even before they are fully vaccinated. Allow your puppy to play freely, but protect him from boisterous puppies and do not allow him to smother timid ones. He needs to learn to play appropriately with dogs of all ages, shapes and sizes, to know when to join

🔼 **Your dog must gently learn about everyday boundaries and what constitutes good behaviour from a very early age.**

▶ **Playing together teaches puppies a wide range of useful social skills.**

in enthusiastically and when to hold back. Adult dogs may discipline him in an effort to teach him better social skills. To assess if your puppy is enjoying the experience separate him from the other dog for a brief moment. If he wants to return to the play session, he is having fun. He needs to be sociable with other dogs, so arrange to meet a variety of different ones on a daily basis.

Plenty of people

Ideally your dog should meet 100 people by the time he is 12 weeks old. Take some treats when you're out together, invite people to your home and hold 'puppy parties'. He must meet a range of people: children, people with beards, hats, sunglasses, uniforms, riding mobility scooters or pushing buggies. If he is nervous or frightened, before he tries to hide or bark, offer him a strongly-scented treat to change what could be a potential threat into an enjoyable encounter.

Environmental socialization

Your dog has to live in a human world, so take him from an early age to busy places: along pavements near traffic and into shops and other public places that allow dogs. Get your puppy accustomed to travelling by public transport as well as by car. Find outdoor cafés and pet shops that will welcome a visit from your dog.

Older dogs

Remedial socialization can help a nervous dog to cope with anxiety and fear disorders and should be implemented with expert assistance through a process of gradual exposure to the stressor concerned.

Other animals

Your dog needs to view other animals he meets, including cats, horses, livestock and deer, with a mild curiosity rather than objects to be feared or chased. Keep him calm and securely on a lead under your control and do not approach them closely.

Handling and grooming

SKILL
LEVEL

Throughout his life, you will have to handle and closely examine your dog regularly, grooming him, checking for fleas, ticks and grass seeds, and looking after him if he is injured or ill. Grooming is essential for maintaining good health and is an enjoyable part of the bonding process between you. It also teaches your dog to stay calm when he is visiting the vet for routine vaccinations and reduces stress if he requires treatment.

Home grooming

You can perform the basic grooming tasks yourself – brushing your dog's coat, trimming his fur and cleaning his ears. Invest in good-quality equipment and always keep brushes and combs scrupulously clean. If your dog has a heavy coat it will need to be brushed every day, especially when he is moulting, and you must set aside enough time for this. A tangled coat can be painful, so don't allow this to happen. Smooth-haired dogs with short coats tend to be low-maintenance and will only need grooming once or twice a week.

◯ Clipping claws is a simple task but be sure not to trim into the 'quick' as it will bleed profusely.

Professional grooming

Some dogs need professional grooming to keep their coats trimmed and in good condition. A good groomer

◗ Collect a suitable grooming kit for your dog, depending on his breed, and invest in good-quality tools for the best results. You may need a grooming rake, stripping comb, clippers and scissors as well as combs, slickers and brushes.

🔺 **Practise handling your dog at home to make your groomer's and vet's jobs easier and far less stressful.**

Dental essentials

Daily brushing is the best way to keep your dog's teeth healthy and clean. Use a long-handled toothbrush with a specially formulated dog toothpaste. It is not only older dogs that can suffer from periodontal disease and tooth decay – young dogs need regular brushing to prevent plaque building up. To promote good oral hygiene, avoid sugary treats and give your dog chews and toys that are designed to keep his teeth clean. Train him to enjoy having his teeth examined and mouth opened by regularly handling this area as you stroke him.

will be happy for you to stay with your dog, so you can reassure him and offer rewards to keep him relaxed. Check that the groomer is qualified and ask whether you can visit before booking the first appointment.

Preparing your dog

Help your groomer to work with your dog by practising at home to prepare him for future visits. Get him used to the sound of clippers and scissors gradually, perhaps while he is otherwise occupied, playing or eating. Lift his feet, one by one, as if clipping his claws, and if he shows signs of uncertainty, distract him with food or a chew toy while you examine him. Use the same distraction and reward techniques if you need to dry his coat with a hairdryer on a low setting. Practise lifting him onto a raised non-slip surface, such as a table covered with a rubber bath mat – this is also a very useful preparation for future visits to your vet.

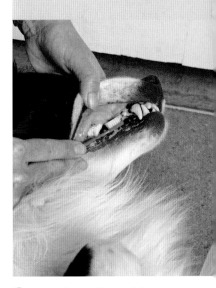

🔺 **Dental care is a quick and simple daily activity that your dog will accept.**

Rescue dogs

If your dog has come from a rescue shelter or has been rehomed privately, you must prepare for his arrival and ongoing needs with great care. He will have experienced great upheavals in his life and will need time and space to adapt to his new home. An older dog will not adjust as rapidly as a puppy and may come with bad habits, which may take time to manifest themselves.

🔺 Rescue dogs may have had a difficult start in life, so make sure you are prepared for the additional time and effort needed. The rewards are immense.

Finding your rescue dog

Ask the staff as many questions as you can about the dog you wish to re-home. A good rescue centre will help you make a suitable choice, so do not feel discouraged if they recommend you wait for a different dog. A good match makes for a happy future for you both, and it is easier to find a compatible temperament by assessing an older dog's behaviour. Look for a non-reactive, laid back temperament if you live in a busy home. If you adopt a challenging dog, be prepared for a rewarding but not always easy experience and work with expert help.

Settling down

Rescue dogs sometimes 'hyper-attach', becoming dependent on their owner's presence, especially if they have experienced traumatic changes. Prevent this by sticking to a normal routine from the moment your dog arrives in your home. This enables him to understand and predict his new boundaries, and relax and settle into his new life more quickly. Stick to regular play, walking and meal times, and do not over-stretch him by expecting him to greet all the visitors who want to meet him. Allow him to interact only when he feels ready, and give him a safe place to retreat to when he wants to be on his own.

Remedial training

Your rescue dog needs to learn the ground rules of his new home, including where to toilet or how to tell you he needs to go out. Take him outside regularly to his toilet area and reward him each time he performs, always giving him your chosen command, such as 'Hurry up'. He will investigate your home thoroughly as he settles and may even chew furniture and items left lying around. Do not leave him unsupervised without providing tasty chew toys. If you are concerned about his behaviour, contact the rescue centre for advice, or arrange to see a qualified, accredited behaviourist to make sure you have a good foundation on which to build a fulfilling relationship.

New and existing dogs

If your rescue dog is intended as a companion for an existing dog, choose one that is compatible. Look for dogs that do not have similar instincts, since this may result in both of them wanting the same life rewards. If they both highly value contact with people, they may squabble over who gets your attention or greets visitors first. Dogs of the opposite sex may get along more amicably if both are neutered, but let them meet several times before making this decision. At home, give each dog his own space and provide additional toys rather than expecting your existing dog to share. This prevents competition over limited resources.

△ Give your dog time to adjust to his new surroundings. He needs to explore and become acclimatized to his new home environment.

▽ Give each dog his own space, own toys and own bed, so they do not feel under pressure to compete.

Skill 5: Stimulation

SKILL
LEVEL

The happiest dogs are busy and stimulated with a balance of daily activities. As a responsible owner, your skill lies in learning how to motivate your dog, find the activities he enjoys and make them part of your everyday routine. When he is keen to work with you, training is much easier – it uses the instincts he naturally possesses to maintain his emotional equilibrium and prevent him becoming stressed or bored. At the same time, you must allow him to just be himself and enjoy things that only a dog can, such as sniffing, digging and rolling in the mud, using his instincts as nature intended.

Exercising your dog in a stimulating place beats boredom and makes daily life much easier, leading to a settled, relaxed pet.

Be attentive

Dogs thrive on attention – it's an important part of your everyday companionship. Be attentive to your dog when he behaves well and calmly, not just when he misbehaves, which may lead to him purposefully doing unwanted things to get your attention. Intermittent attention can lead to problem behaviour, so you must be consistent.

Involve the family

Your dog is part of your extended family and they will have to look after him occasionally. Teach everyone how to work with him – he will detect even the tiniest inconsistency and this will help him to learn subtle differences in their handling skills. Take him to a training class that welcomes family involvement – everyone can benefit from the same information and advice.

Games and jobs

All training should be enjoyable, but categorizing tasks according to purpose means some games are played for enjoyment whereas others promote a useful job. Training your dog to do tasks around the house helps involve him and teaches him behaviours you want to encourage, such as emptying the washing machine or fetching the telephone handset. Tricks are a relaxing way of training him, even though they may not be particularly useful.

Beat boredom

Dogs with too little to do may become stressed and destructive. If they are confined, they may chew and nibble at themselves, or develop compulsive disorders, including unremitting barking or tail chasing. The level of activity needed to prevent boredom varies depending on your dog's age and breed. An adolescent dog has boundless energy compared to an older dog. A Siberian Husky or Springer Spaniel needs a great deal of physical exercise compared to a Bichon Frise or a Newfoundland. There are exceptions, so get to know what your own dog needs, bearing in mind that some days he will be more active than others. Regular play with other dogs will also help maintain his fitness and social health.

Independent friends

Although your dog is your companion he should be able to cope without your physical presence. If you have to constantly reassure and seek contact with him, he may become anxious when you inevitably have to go out. Keep a balance between the time you spend with your dog and the time he spends alone. You do not have to entertain him every minute of the day.

⬤ **Find a well-qualified, experienced dog trainer and attend classes with your dog.**

Time to rest

Dogs tend to mix bursts of activity with long periods of sleep, and hyperactive ones often need some quiet time. Your dog may race around madly at certain times of the day (usually in the early evening) or may seem insistent on mouthing and pestering you when nothing seems to satisfy him. These are signs of overtiredness, so give him some time to rest on his own in a calm, non-stimulating place.

SKILL
LEVEL

Fun games to play with your dog

Games may seem unproductive but they represent a relaxed way to teach your dog new skills and for him to learn about you. Tricks are no different from any other training exercise apart from their intended purpose. Give him time to learn; if mistakes occur, change something you're doing until he gets it right.

Teaching your dog to fetch can become a useful skill that he will enjoy.

Fetch

Begin by playing with your dog with a soft toy that he can easily hold in his mouth but with enough of it hanging down for you to take it without getting caught by his teeth as he moves. Sit on the floor facing a corner of the room to prevent him escaping and encourage him to play in the gap between you and the corner. Keep the toy low to the ground. Just as he is about to grab it, toss it into the corner and excitedly encourage him to pick it up. As soon as it is in his mouth, give your cue word: 'Fetch!' Pat your legs and clap your hands to encourage him to bring it back to you immediately. If he tries to dodge past you, attach a houseline or lead to his collar to gently dissuade him. Repeat a few times, and then end the game. If he holds onto the toy, teach him to swap it for a treat or another toy.

Hide and seek games build a powerful recall and also keep your dog alert to your whereabouts.

🐾 **Hunting for a toy is an exciting and useful game that can be adapted to find lost items, such as car keys!**

Search for a toy

While you are playing with your dog, rather than throwing the toy for him to fetch, quickly go and hide it in an obvious place, such as poking out from under a cushion. Tell him to fetch and, as he does so, say, 'Find it!' Praise and reward him well when he reaches the toy. Next time, hide it in the same place but tuck it further in underneath the cushion and repeat 'Find it!' Praise him each time he reaches the item, and play with him as a reward when he brings it back to you.

Hide and seek

Ask your dog to stay or get a family member to hold his collar. Race excitedly away from him, while he watches, and hide in the same room. At first make your hiding place obvious, so he rushes over to you the moment he is released. Repeat, but each time make your hiding place less visible. Play this game around the garden and even when out on walks. It is an excellent way of perfecting your dog's recall skill as he will always keep an eye on you, thinking that you are likely to vanish at any point.

Magic moments

Combine some fun games with the tricks on pages 64–65 and ask your dog to wave his 'magic paw'. When practising, teach him to fetch a specific toy that you always put in the same place on the floor. Tell your guests that your dog can read. Scatter some other toys on the ground around the 'special toy' (not too close). Write the name of the toy on a piece of paper and show it to your dog as if he is 'reading'. When you send him to fetch, he will go straight to his favourite toy and bring it back to you.

SKILL
LEVEL

Easy tricks and household tasks

Teach your dog some jobs he can enjoy helping with around the house. Use a clicker to signal that he is performing the desired behaviour correctly (your click should come at the exact moment he does the right thing), or use verbal signals, such as 'Good dog!' After each success, offer a treat to motivate him to continue. As he becomes more experienced, you won't need to use frequent treats because the task itself, and your happy reaction, will be sufficient motivation. Keep the sessions short and fun, and always finish on a success.

⚠ **A dog can have his own doorbell, ringing it to attract your attention when he needs to go out to toilet.**

Fetch the post

Once you have taught your dog to do a 'play fetch' (see page 62), ask him to fetch some scrap paper inside a sealed envelope, but don't let him get over-excited, trying to tear the paper. Practise this until he can fetch and carry the envelope without damaging it. Next, ask someone to post it through the letterbox and practise again. Progress gradually with different sized packages and envelopes until he will fetch the post for you on command.

Ring the bell to go out

Teach your dog to signal that he wants to toilet outside with this fun exercise. You will need some bells that are securely attached to a rope or ribbon on a door handle.

1 Place a treat underneath the bell, so your dog has to push the bell out of the way to get to it. Add your cue word, 'Outside', as he does this. Always praise him well.
2 Say 'Outside' when he is some distance away from the bell, so that he runs to it and nudges it on your cue.
3 When he has mastered this, hang the bell on a door handle within easy reach and repeat the command. Treat him after you praise him or click and treat each success.
4 Next, as he rings the bell, open the door and toss the treat outside. He will begin anticipating that ringing the bell means he can go out. Place some treats outside in readiness and send him from further away.
5 Finally, withhold the treat until he runs to the bell, rings it, goes outside and toilets, and then reward him.

Wave a paw

Ask your dog to sit (for stability), then gently lift one of his front paws and, as you do so, say 'Wave', 'Good dog', or click the clicker. Give him a treat and let him put his paw back down on the ground. Repeat several times in quick succession until he begins to anticipate you and lifts his paw as you say 'Wave' and your hand reaches down. Gradually change the reaching hand to a waving movement, and repeat until you can lift your hand into a wave signal. Now your dog can greet, and say goodbye, to visitors, in a more suitable way than jumping up!

Tidy up toys

As your dog returns a toy, place a box under your hand, so he drops it in. Initially, this will happen by accident, but by placing a food reward inside the box immediately after he drops the toy he will target the box to get his treat. Next place the box further away and repeat the training. With careful timing, he will learn to add toys to the box in order to earn a treat. Practise this daily and he will start to tidy his toys away in anticipation of edible rewards.

Empty the machine!

You can extend the tidying up toys training to teach your dog to pull washing out of the machine and place it in a basket; he will feel very important to be entrusted with such a useful chore.

◑ Tidying up gives you a clean floor as well as a fulfilled, interested dog.

SKILL
LEVEL

Use your dog's natural talents

Harness your dog's natural instincts and behaviour to make him happy. Hunting, retrieving, herding and games can keep a dog in good mental and physical health, but not all dogs have an energetic talent – some have been bred for companionship. Occasionally a dog's natural instinct can lead to problems and It's your job to provide fun tasks that channel his instincts into useful activities. He won't reach his full potential without your help.

Tugging safely

Bull breeds, like Staffords, enjoy tugging games with a toy, but these must be under your control to strict rules.

1 Make sure you teach an instant 'release' command.

2 Use an item you can easily retrieve, such as a 1.2m (4ft) length of broom handle, which keeps your fingers safely out of harm's way.

3 Only allow your dog to tug when you give him the specific command.

4 If he snatches at you, jumps up uninvited or his teeth touch your skin, stop immediately and retrain at a lower intensity when he calms down.

Gundog games

Your gundog has been bred to perform specific tasks that involve retrieving, hunting and pointing, but they all need human guidance. Traditionally, Labradors and Retrievers fetch, Spaniels hunt for, flush out and retrieve game, and Setters and Pointers indicate its location by freezing in a 'point' position. Teach your dog to indicate where the toys you throw land, to hunt for them when they are hidden in long grass, and return them to you.

Dig it!

Terriers love to dig; their proportionately large feet make expert spades, and their instinct to find vermin means that they dig to seek prey. If your dog has these

⊙ **Agility not only builds up your handling skill but is also enjoyable teamwork for both you and your dog.**

tendencies, consider constructing a digging pit in an unused area of your garden or hide some of his toys inside cardboard boxes for him to dig into and retrieve.

Built for speed

Border Collies and other really active dogs tend to learn new tasks extremely quickly (needing only one or two repetitions). With their sensitive hearing and excellent sight, they are high-performance dogs for experienced owners. Your Border Collie puppy needs huge amounts of stimulation and exercise, with plenty of direction from you, so enrol him in a training class without delay. At around 12 months of age, you can specialize with agility or obedience work, or even begin working trials in order to develop his hunting and tracking instincts.

Hounds that sniff

Beagles and Bloodhounds have the best scenting ability. If your Hound is easily distracted out walking, try leaving an object behind you and then teach him to go back and look for it. Start with something large, such as an old glove or sock, and then shrink it down gradually in size to a fabric key ring with your scent on it. Once your dog is regularly finding this, attach your keys to the ring and if you ever drop them when you're out on a walk, you know who to ask to retrieve them! Your dog will enjoy using his natural scenting abilities and being useful, too.

Gundogs will benefit from playing games in which their hunt – point – retrieve natural instincts enable them to excel.

Play tug games with small dogs following strict rules; always make sure your dog lets go immediately on command.

A sight hound's exceptional detection of movement means he can spot small prey from a great distance away and may give chase at amazing speeds.

Nose work for all

Any dog can be taught to use his nose with a tracking and searching activity. Lay a track by walking alone across some undisturbed ground, leaving toys or food pots for your dog to find at set places along the route. At first, mark the track with poles to help you to gauge your dog's tracking progress. Keep it straight, making a note of landmarks, such as trees, and draw the route plan in a notebook. Leave the biggest reward at the end of the track. Your dog will enjoy following your scent and finding the items. As he gets more proficient, lay longer tracks and attach a harness and line to walk behind him. If you both enjoy this, you can even enter Working Trial competitions where his tracking ability will be put to the test.

Special sight

A usually calm Greyhound changes dramatically when he sees a sudden movement. Sight hounds can be difficult to control once they are chasing squirrels or rabbits, so do not permit this. They may see a cat or small dog and chase this instead, not realizing their mistake until it's too late. Use your dog's instincts to chase toys, especially ones thrown along the ground: these are within your control and give him the chance to enjoy his exercise.

Gentle giants

Giant breeds, such as the Newfoundland, were used as carting or 'draft' dogs. Their strength and size means they can pull heavy loads, and even jump from boats to pull people to safety. Clubs exist for this specialized training, and competitions are organized to test the dogs' skills. Teach your dog to use his strength for a useful purpose, but check first that he is physically fit.

Crossbreeds

A strong working instinct can also be found in many crossbreeds, especially those descended from Labrador

Retrievers, Springer Spaniels, Border Collies, German Shepherd Dogs and terriers. Your dog may be a mixture of breeds, but even if you do not know his exact heritage you can still develop activities to access his instinctive needs. Try to assess his energy levels, the activities he enjoys and his willingness to be active. If he is always on the go or getting into mischief, try out a new activity together, such as tracking, obedience work or agility.

⚪ **Crossbreeds may have a mixture of instincts and need fulfilling activities.**

⚪ **Your dog will enjoy obedience training and working as part of a team with you. Make it fun!**

Building concentration

You can harness your dog's instincts, whatever his breed, if he likes being busy, through obedience work, which is more precise than everyday teaching. Formal obedience training, far from suppressing his instincts, can help him develop close concentration, so he follows your actions. He learns to focus on every detail of his own movement, too, fine-tuning his valuable sensory awareness. Exercises include close heelwork, send-aways, control at a distance and scent work. Obedience also involves sit and down stay training, which can be a welcome break for you. The objective is to occupy him in a positive way as too much pressure can have a deleterious effect.

Sports and activities

SKILL
LEVEL

From formal obedience exercises to just plain fun, your dog can join in a range of activities with you as part of a team. Through participating in the selection of sports on offer, you can learn to work in harmony together. Your dog may need to be a certain age or have attained a level of fitness for some, but most canine sports are intended to include all ages and abilities, so give them a try. You will find something enjoyable that suits both of you.

Rally-O

In Rally Obedience (Rally-O or Rally), each dog and handler navigate a course consisting of 10–20 signs giving specific actions, such as 'send over jump', 'sit down sit', 'left turn' and so on. Handlers can talk to their dogs and encourage them throughout whilst the dogs remain in the heel position between signs. This is great fun for everyone.

Flyball

Flyball is a relay race with four dogs in two teams competing against one another at the same time. The course consists of a starting line, four hurdles spaced a set distance apart and a 'flyball box' (usually a spring-loaded box that releases a tennis ball) per team. The hurdle height is dependent on the height of the dogs. Each dog jumps the hurdles and steps on the flyball box to release the ball, which he grabs before running back over the hurdles. When he crosses the starting line it is the turn of the next dog in the team.

Agility

Agility is an obstacle course for a dog and handler working together. The handler directs the dog around, over and through jumps, tunnels, walkways and the

Weaving poles in agility are initially taught by bending the poles outwards in this way.

🔵 **Obstacles can give your dog confidence in his body movement, and dog sports enable both of you to become fitter and work together as a true team.**

infamous weave poles in a numbered order decided by the judge. The round is timed and faults are awarded for failure to complete the obstacles correctly, or in the wrong order. Handlers are not allowed to touch their dog nor the obstacles and the dog must run freely without any kind of lead.

CaniX

CaniX, or Canicross, is the sport of running with your dog. You can use a normal collar and lead or a specially designed harness whereby the dog is attached to his owner via an elasticated running line and can pull him or her comfortably. Events are available for all breeds and different levels of fitness.

Obedience competition

Competitive Obedience consists of a set of formal exercises that the dog and handler must complete with extreme precision. Heelwork, Recall, Retrieve, Sendaway, Distant control, Scent discrimination and Stays all form part of the tests involved. Levels of competition reflect experience and accuracy, and judges mark faults when scoring, so the lower the score, the better the performance.

🔵 **Obedience exercises rely on precise control on the part of both your dog and you, his handler.**

Skill 6: Awareness

SKILL
LEVEL

As dogs grow, their needs change enormously, and you must develop the skills and patience that all responsible owners need for each development stage. Your new puppy requires considerable time as well as a social and financial investment. Your adolescent dog is developing his individual characteristics and needs special guidance from you as he matures. Your adult dog must be kept active and busy with a daily routine and regular monitoring. And your elderly dog will need special consideration as his mind and body age to keep him healthy and prevent him becoming distressed or disorientated.

△ Young puppies bond with their owners quickly and rely on them for guidance and teaching, as well as protection.

Be aware of changes

As your dog grows older, you may not realize that he is reaching some important stages in his life. He will pass through many learning phases and you must be ready to prevent him making mistakes – for instance, through hormonal changes that may cause him to react differently to other dogs. He needs socialization and training as a puppy and adolescent, and he will require reminders throughout his life to keep these skills fresh.

How long does each stage last?

On average, smaller dogs mature faster and live longer than larger breeds. The old adage of 'dog years' (one dog year equates to seven human ones) does not reflect the complexity of this relationship. A large breed puppy, such as a Great Dane, is still growing rapidly and could be considered a junior dog until he is two years old.

Challenges of dog ownership

Life stages require understanding and patience on your part. The most challenging times are only temporary, like the chewing phase or toilet training of a puppy, or the exuberant and pushy adolescent stages. Your dog is just as new to these experiences as you and may feel fearful when his behaviour is difficult. To cope with these challenges, set your expectations to fit with his life stage.

⚠ Expect your adult dog to rely on his regular daily routine to maintain his physical and mental wellbeing.

Behaviour expectations

Make sure you give your dog clear, fair boundaries, such as not allowing him to jump up at people no matter what his age. Attach a lead to his collar for additional control while teaching him, and attend training classes for as long as possible to learn practical skills together. Unwanted behaviour escalates through the life stages and is often a sign of more problems to come – do not ignore it. Intervene immediately and calmly when he exhibits excitable activity, such as barking, and don't give him the opportunity to continue. Teach him to look at you for instruction instead. Always avoid harsh training as this does not establish boundaries.

Nutritional needs

Adapt your feeding plan according to your dog's needs. A young puppy should eat frequent, small meals of a good-quality puppy food. His nutrient requirements differ from those of adult dogs – more protein and enough food to meet his additional energy needs. Large breeds require interim 'junior' nutrition to support the increased time taken to reach their adult body weight. A five-month old Chihuahua weighing 1kg (2lb) has different calorific needs (250 kcal per day) to an Irish Wolfhound of the same age who weighs 30kg (66lb) and needs 3,200 kcal.

Special diets

At all stages, keep your dog's food intake balanced and stable, and consider making dietary changes or a special diet if he suffers from skin, digestive or other health problems. Ask your vet for advice or consult a qualified canine nutritionist. Older dogs have lower energy requirements than younger ones and they may need a special reduced-calorie diet that is designed to keep their joints healthy, too.

⚠ Adolescent stages can often be the most challenging as your dog's behaviour goes through noticeable changes.

SKILL
LEVEL

Puppy life stages

A puppy's life stages progress rapidly and there is a lot to do within the first few months. Your puppy learned to wag his tail, vocalize with barks and growls, and notice the world around him when he was only two weeks old. By four weeks, his eyesight was almost as well developed as that of an adult dog, and he could hear and orientate himself, too. Playful behaviour is a characteristic of domestic dogs of all ages – they are neotenized (their juvenile characteristics are retained into adult life). However, there are some important aspects of your puppy's behaviour that will diminish as he ages.

▲ Mildly exciting events are part of the routine of socializing your puppy, but always be careful to keep the sessions short and fun rather than overwhelming.

Mouthing and chewing

Puppies explore with their mouths, using chewing and mouthing, and their pin-sharp teeth come into contact with everything around them. They do not behave maliciously, so patience and re-direction onto suitable, safe and tasty dog toys are key. Your puppy is not deliberately trying to spoil your household and you must not punish him for this instinctive and normal behaviour.

Puppy manners

Your puppy must learn good manners and you should promote relaxed, confident interactions, discouraging excitability by always staying calm and distracting him. Although you have to expect him to make some mistakes

Socialization

Provide pleasant encounters for your puppy with as many people, animals and situations as possible during the crucial developmental stage between eight and eleven weeks. If he has not been fully vaccinated, you can carry him in public and he can still experience everyday challenges and the mild stressors that will help to build a confident adult. Never put him under extreme pressure as any extremely fearful event will stay with him for the remainder of his life.

🔺 A crate provides a safe and welcoming den for your puppy as well as helping with your housetraining routine and preventing inappropriate chewing.

you should make a point of not allowing him to repeat them. This may take extra vigilance and effort on your part but it is much easier to get this right by putting in the foundation time at a young age than to try and correct a learned bad habit later in life.

Training classes

To find a good puppy training class in your area, ask the staff at your veterinary clinic and local pet shop staff or talk to other dog owners. Always visit the class before taking your puppy along for the first time. Classes should be fun for both of you as well as pushing you and your dog to the best of your abilities. Talk to the trainers and assess their approach, taking care to find out whether they use kind, fair methods, have kept their skills up to date and are qualified and registered with a leading organization. Be prepared to spend some time practising what you learn to obtain the best results and recognize that you must continue training your dog throughout his life. If you have any concerns, discuss them with your trainer – it is their role to help you get on the right track.

Crates and pens

Puppies who are given too much freedom at home can learn bad habits as they roam freely, toileting and chewing wherever they wish. A safe puppy crate or pen enables you to safely leave your dog for short periods and teaches him that being alone is not a frightening experience. It is a retreat where he can get adequate rest in a bustling home where children may not appreciate that a young animal needs time and space alone. It also becomes a portable den for car journeys and visits to people's homes, and you can even take it on holiday. Consider it an investment in your puppy's safety and future, not a punishment or prison.

🔺 Providing appropriate chew items is essential; all puppies need to chew!

House-training your puppy

Puppies learn to leave their nest to eliminate elsewhere. House-training is an extension of this behaviour, but your puppy may not automatically want to go outside to toilet. Cold weather, rain and darkness can be intimidating and he may wait to toilet until he is back indoors where he feels relaxed. If he has previously been house-trained and develops toileting problems, check it out with your vet.

⬆ **Take your puppy outside at regular intervals and reward him when he toilets to avoid future problems.**

Toileting routine

Successful toilet training depends upon confinement and supervision. Establish a routine and minimize mistakes by taking your puppy outside every 30 minutes. Use a command, such as 'Hurry up', each time he toilets, followed by a food treat. Punishing him for accidents in the house is unacceptable as it reflects incomplete training on your part. Ignore his mistakes and be more vigilant next time. Clean the area with a specially-formulated product – ammonia-based cleaners do not break down the bacteria in the same way as biological ones and may attract him back to the same spot.

⬇ **At first you may need to accompany your puppy outside and encourage him, as he may not have the confidence to toilet alone.**

Celebrate successes

Once your puppy has toileted, reward him with freedom
to play and investigate. He will soon need to toilet again,
especially after playing, eating, drinking or sleeping. Use
a crate or house line to monitor him and react quickly to
the telltale signs: usually an urgent sniffing and circling
movement. Go outside with him in all weathers, wait
patiently and reward him each time, so that he actually
enjoys the process and eventually will ask to go out.

Fear of outdoors

Young puppies can feel the cold, especially if they have
not developed their full coat. A puppy jacket will keep
your dog warm and dry during the winter. Make walks
fun by taking some treats, and encourage your puppy
if he hangs back or tries to hide behind you. Engage his
hunting instinct by laying a trail of tiny treats to start
him moving. Encourage his enthusiasm and make walks
enjoyable, so he trots at your side without dragging.

Follow your lead

Your puppy needs a flat collar or harness and lead for
walks, but he may be frightened initially of the unfamiliar
sensation of restraint and will pull away from any tension
on his lead. Before taking him out, attach his lead and
allow him to trail it around the house and garden under
your supervision. Hold the lead and call him to you whilst
crouching down, holding a toy or treat. Pull gently as he
moves to teach him that a taut lead is not to be feared.

⬥ **Allow your puppy to
trail his lead in the garden
to get him used to the
unfamiliar sensation.**

Puppies welcome

Help your puppy become
part of your community
by visiting suitable shops,
outdoor cafés and garden
centres while he is still very
young. As well as assisting
his social learning, it will
also create a good reception
in later life when he will be
recognized and welcomed.
Keep your visits short as his
attention span is limited
and he requires frequent
rests at this age. Take some
treats and water with you,
along with a tasty chew toy.
If someone holds or strokes
him, use the chew toy to
distract his mouth to prevent
him nipping playfully at their
hands, face or clothing.

Adolescent life stages

SKILL
LEVEL

Encouraging good habits must continue throughout your dog's life, but this is never more important than during their adolescent years. Being a 'teenager' can be a difficult time, especially for juvenile males. Your dog may become rebellious, disobedient and pushy, but don't worry – this is just a passing phase and it will be more manageable if you look upon it from his perspective.

🔺 A trailing line will give you more control over your adolescent dog if he fails to obey commands and runs off instead.

What happens in adolescence?

At 18 weeks, your dog is nearing the end of the puppy stages. Hormonal changes will cause a male dog to cock his leg to urinate while a bitch will be approaching her first season. As your older puppy becomes more independent, adult behaviours, such as hunting further afield, chasing rabbits and investigating other dogs through sniffing their rear ends, will become apparent. Your male dog may behave in a more confrontational manner with other males, and squabbles are common.

Maintaining social confidence

Adolescence is the time when dogs lose confidence in social situations. They go through a number of 'fear periods', often coinciding with unpleasant or novel experiences and leaving them with an aversion or long-term anxiety. To prevent this, take your dog out regularly to play with familiar playmates, while allowing him to investigate new situations and greet new people. You've worked hard at his socialization during puppyhood but he will forget these skills if you isolate him at this age.

Independence and reliability

Your compliant puppy has changed into a more self-reliant dog who wants to run off and investigate at greater distances. Commands you have taught him may suddenly no longer work as he chooses whether or not to obey. The solution is to spot mistakes early on and never allow them to become a habit. If your adolescent dog fails to come back when you call him, just attach a long 10m (30ft) line to his collar and allow him to trail it along behind him, so that you can easily reinforce your training when you next call him. Keep up your formal recall training and do not assume that he is just trying to be naughty – a lot of supposed disobedient behaviour is caused by insufficient or inconsistent teaching.

Sexual changes and neutering

You are likely to witness more sexually dimorphic behaviours (specific to your dog being physically male or female). A male dog will lift his leg to urinate, not just for toileting purposes but also to leave his scent. A bitch may come into season, which may not only affect her appetite and coat condition but also her mood, as she becomes more clingy or grumpy. She may flirt with male dogs by drawing her tail to one side. If you are not planning to breed from your dog, get him or her neutered; ask your vet about the best age for this. You may see behavioural changes as a result of neutering although these are not guaranteed, and if you plan to neuter your dog as a result of problem behaviour, speak with a qualified behaviourist first. Sometimes, neutering for behavioural reasons can be disappointing or, at worst, counterproductive as it may exacerbate the problem you are trying to prevent.

⬣ **Scent marking is normal behaviour outdoors, but not indoors, so stay vigilant.**

⬣ **Adolescents may challenge you as they learn, refusing to do things they did as puppies, such as letting go in tug games. Reinforce your dog's training and be patient.**

Challenges

Your adolescent dog will begin to challenge your boundaries, but you must stay calm and persist with your original training plan. A disobedient teenager needs clear guidance without confrontation as he is probably exploring what he can and cannot get away with. If you respond aggressively, this will frighten him and will not teach him anything other than that you behave unpredictably and in a scary way. Do not allow the good bond you established in puppyhood to break down in this way – persist and insist.

Adult life stages

SKILL
LEVEL

Your dog has now settled into his adult routine and you can relax some of the physical boundaries you have imposed when he stops chewing. However, you must keep his life as busy and fulfilled as before, rather than being tempted to slow down a little. Continue letting him mix with other dogs and people, and adopt a forward-thinking attitude to any problems that may develop.

⬆ **Adult dogs are often more settled but they still need plenty of stimulation.**

⬇ **Walk your dog in different places to provide enjoyable experiences.**

Assessing your dog

Your adult dog may delight and annoy you in equal measure as he greets you with gentle enthusiasm one moment and knocks you over the next. The time has come to assess his adult personality and to realize that his best qualities are also likely to be his least endearing. For instance, if he is naturally quiet and laid back, he will not steal food or jump up at visitors, but, equally, he may not be easy to motivate when it comes to training. If he never leaves your side when out on walks and has an enviable recall, he may suffer from anxiety when you are not around. A friendly, sociable dog may always rush away from you to play with other dogs and greet people unless you step in and control him. Take a philosophical approach by realizing that no dog can be perfect, but deal swiftly with problems that appear to be escalating. Accept your dog's personality, control the excess, and enjoy the features that make him your individual pet.

◀ Puzzle toys will keep your adult dog stimulated and busy; they can even be used to feed him his dinner.

Making life interesting

There are lots of positive ways of stimulating your dog and making his life more enjoyable. Why not consider joining a more advanced training class or perhaps trying a dog sport, such as agility or flyball (see pages 70–71)? You might want to teach him a simple party trick that you both enjoy performing, or give him a job to do to make him feel involved, such as picking up dropped clothes pegs or fetching items (see pages 62–63). Even if you do not want to train him formally, you can provide stimulation by walking him in new and interesting locations, such as in the countryside or on the beach.

Going places with your dog

In some countries dogs accompany their owners to most public places and are positively welcomed. Well-behaved dogs in public can be a good conversation-starter, so do not neglect taking your dog out with you whenever possible. This helps to maintain the socialization work you have put in place, as dogs do not retain this learning forever without regular reminders.

Enjoying companionship

This is the stage of your dog's life that you will most cherish, so take time to just be together and enjoy the companionship that he offers. Toys and games that involve problem-solving are a particularly good way to bond quietly with him as well as fine-tuning your understanding of his body language and signals.

'Puppy-helpers'

If your adult dog is really well socialized and tolerant, why not ask the staff at your dog training club whether they need a calm adult dog to help with puppy classes? Owners are often nervous about allowing their puppies to meet adult dogs in case they do not get on well together. Alternatively, you may wish to register your dog as a therapy dog to visit hospitals, day centres and care homes. This can be very rewarding voluntary work for both of you, and he will enjoy being stroked and fussed over and making people feel good.

Elderly life stages

SKILL
LEVEL

Now your dog is advancing in years, this new stage of his life brings its own considerations for his environment and needs. He may become reliant on you for his security and comfort, and there may be inconveniences, but ultimately this is a rewarding time when you can strengthen the bond between you.

The long goodbye

Your old dog may begin waking at night for no reason or bark incessantly when he is left alone, showing classic signs of separation anxiety. He may begin toileting indoors, and even do so in front of you, as if he no longer remembers to go outside. He might show reduced recognition of familiar people or a general lack of enthusiasm and will sleep a lot. These are all symptoms of cognitive dysfunction, so consult your vet, who may even refer you to an accredited behaviourist for support. Food supplements can be helpful as well as a routine that prevents him becoming distressed and disorientated.

What is old age?

Although a dog is classed as geriatric at seven years, this varies according to breed, size and general health. The average life expectancy is 13 years, but giant breeds tend to live less and small breeds considerably more than this. You may not notice that your dog is approaching old age since it is a gradual decline and his needs may not be obvious. Regularly assess his general health and if you suspect he is starting to 'slow down', becoming grumpy or getting forgetful, consult your vet. He may have an age-related disorder that can be treated.

Failing senses

Elderly dogs need special consideration as their senses are not as sharp as they once were. Dogs usually compensate for the loss of one sense, such as hearing, but old dogs may have failing sight as well, or a combination of other

▶ Older dogs need regular health checks, and showing regard for their slower pace will keep them fulfilled.

physical problems. Give yours extra time to eat, take care when moving around him, and if you have to move any furniture, supervise him while he learns the new layout.

○ Even if your old dog's senses are diminished, he will still love going for an interesting walk.

Exercise and activity

Your dog may not want to compete with younger ones and might growl or snap if they play too roughly. If so, call them away and allow him to seek them out when he wants to play. He may still enjoy walks but more frequent, shorter ones, at a more sedate pace and over easier, flatter terrain. Let him race around if that's what he enjoys – it will help keep him active and at a healthy weight. Consider getting him a warm coat for cold or wet weather to keep his temperature even.

Physical health

You must take care not to allow your senior dog to get overweight. This places a strain on his joints and can age him beyond his years due to the health complications that obesity causes. Switch his food to one for older dogs that is lower in fat and protein. Cut down on snacks and titbits and make them a weekly, rather than a daily, treat. Look out for excessive water drinking as this can be a sign of more serious underlying health problems.

○ Most old dogs can compensate for physical problems with other senses.

Skill 7: Responsibility

You have responsibilities as an owner not only to protect and nurture your dog – to ensure he is socialized around other dogs and people and behaves well with good manners in public – but also to provide a secure and happy home. You need to give him your time, attention, companionship, a regular routine and stability as well as keeping him fit and healthy in body and mind. Your skill here is to take a long-term view of responsible ownership: predicting possible pitfalls, familiarizing yourself with risks and taking proactive measures to deal with any problems that arise, long before they become unmanageable.

Respect is mutual

Your dog's ability to learn from you is well adapted, but you cannot hope for him to understand human laws or predict some events and outcomes. This is your role as his protector and teacher. Equally, do not blame yourself if he fails to follow 'human rules'; make a mental note of the situation and take steps to prevent problems recurring.

⚠ **Doorways can become a real danger, so you must train your dog to sit calmly and not to dash out.**

Setting rules and boundaries

Teach your dog a set of basic rules – be consistent and stick to them. Simply teaching him to wait at an open door, for example, is a safe choice he can easily learn but only with your help. Respect the level of learning and understanding he can achieve. Show him and reward the behaviour you want, and always be fair, kind and consistent in maintaining these boundaries.

Home safety

You may not realize how many potential hazards exist in your home until your dog arrives. Consider how he may interpret his new environment and which areas may pose a risk. A 'dog's eye view' of your house and garden must be based on his specific instincts and play styles, such as attractive chew items based on their scent and texture. Establish a safe area where you can leave him when you are away from home or unable to supervise him.

🔺 Greeting new people can be fun, but remember that you are responsible for your dog when he's out in public, so always supervise him carefully.

Parties

At family celebrations and parties, visitors may leave drinks and food where your dog can reach them. Boxes of chocolate or sweet-tasting alcohol are particular concerns. If you cannot supervise your dog, consider keeping him in his quiet space once he has greeted everyone. He may find the event more stressful than you think, so this may be the best solution for everyone.

Public liability

Legislation regarding dogs in public places is increasingly strict, so be aware of national laws as well as local ones. Some parks may not allow dogs to roam freely off the lead where there are children's playgrounds, and beaches are sometimes closed to dogs at peak times of the year. Socialize your dog thoroughly and teach him to sit when an unfamiliar person approaches, especially children.

Fitness and health

Invest in good outdoor clothing and footwear, as your dog relies on you for daily exercise and this will be in all weathers. Find walks that you both enjoy and that have a good variety of experiences in store. Keep your dog physically in good health as well as in good behavioural health and maintain a balance between the two; good nutrition, regular exercise and regular social contact with other dogs and people should be part of your dog's everyday life. Regular visits to your vet are essential if disease and illnesses are to be prevented.

🔺 Fit dogs have a reduced risk of obesity and disease.

Safety in your home

SKILL
LEVEL

Your dog needs to chew throughout his puppyhood and this will continue until he is at least a year old. His jaws were originally designed to chew through animal hide, so he can do a great deal of damage in a very short space of time. Never leave expensive shoes and trainers lying around, and always close cupboard doors securely, especially if they contain toxic household detergents and cleaning agents.

Safety solutions

Dog-proof your home, switching off live electric sockets at ground level, hooking trailing wires out of the way and raising blinds and curtains off the floor. When you cannot supervise your dog, put him in a room where his chewing will result in only limited damage. Use wastebins with pop-up, not swing, lids to stop him accessing sharp edges on cans or ingesting unwanted items. Use stairgates on doorways to give you instant control. Place a fireguard around open fires as your dog may easily singe his tail.

🔺 **If your dog is naturally inquisitive, don't leave any potentially harmful items within his reach.**

Edible dangers

Human scent is particularly motivating for dogs, so TV remote controls and phone handsets are at risk as well as socks and shoes. Any item you wear or touch regularly may tempt your dog, so keep them of reach. If you leave him alone in the kitchen, put any cleaning products away and empty mop buckets. Store medications in secure

◀ **A good-quality waste bin with a secure lid that your dog cannot open will reduce the likelihood of bin-raiding activity.**

containers in drawers or cupboards. Sports bags and handbags can contain hazardous items, so don't leave them lying around. Hang up your bags and coats.

Door safety

Your dog must learn that doors are only for access to permitted places. A front door opens on to many hazards – traffic and people who may not welcome a dog running towards them. Never allow him to push ahead of you through a door unless you give a release command. Attach a lead to his collar as you open the door, and do not let him move from that spot. Teach him that he can only go through when you give him a verbal command. This allows you to move in and out of all doorways whilst he remains away from the door. A dog trained thoroughly in this skill will not attempt to go through any door, no matter who opens it and even if it is accidentally left ajar.

Theft risks

Sadly, dogs are at risk of theft and you should ensure your house is securely locked and fenced, especially if you have a rare or popular breed. A dog flap opening into the garden can provide a temptation for burglars as well as making your dog an easier target for thieves.

Chew temptations

Be aware of the following if your dog enjoys chewing:

Texture – fabric, wood and soft plastic

Examples – cushions, table legs, electric cable coating

Scent – Items from outdoors, touched by hands, things worn regularly and food

Examples – outdoor shoes, TV remote control, mobile phone, slippers

Sound – paper, plastic bags and children's toys

Examples – newspapers, sandwich wrappers, rattles, electronic games

⬆ **Stair gates provide an excellent security barrier whilst you are teaching your dog not to jump up or dash out.**

SKILL
LEVEL

Garden and outdoor safety

Many common garden plants can be poisonous to your dog if they are eaten in significant quantities. Seemingly innocuous foliage, berries, seeds and even the bulbs of plants such as the humble Daffodil can prove fatally toxic, so check out the plants in your garden and any areas where you walk your dog.

Public hygiene

The task of clearing up your dog's faeces is a legal responsibility in public places, and bags that are specially designed for this purpose are available, along with containers to store them in until you reach a suitable disposal site. Never leave full bags behind; even biodegradeable bags take a long time to decompose and they look unsightly, so clean up after your dog.

Gardening compromises

Recently disturbed earth is attractive to most dogs and may result in them digging up plants and bulbs. To avoid this, plant them in raised beds or containers or use green plastic-coated chicken wire mesh to fence off areas you wish to protect. You will still be able to enjoy your garden whilst preventing trampling and urine damage to foliage. Place 'closer' springs on all garden gates to make certain that these cannot be left open accidentally. Add a 'Keep Gate Closed' sign for additional security.

Dry areas for wet times

During inclement weather your lawn may become muddy and it will be difficult for grass to grow if your dog plays on this area daily. Urine can also burn grass and leave bare patches on your pristine lawn. Consider investing in a practical hard-surfaced area with a fenced edging to allow the grass to re-establish itself and use part of it as a

◐ Keep garden chemicals safely shut away and read the labels carefully to make sure that they are safe for use around pets. Some common garden fertilizers, such as bonemeal, can be very appealing to dogs but they must not be eaten.

🔺 **Concrete flooring in an outside run is simple to keep clean and is sometimes a good investment.**

dog toilet. This area can be made to look attractive with planted containers and is easy to keep clean and hygienic by frequent rinsing with kennel disinfectant.

Diverting digging

Digging is a natural and enjoyable activity for your dog. If he enjoys digging up the lawn and plants, provide him with his own special digging area surrounded by slabs that can easily be tidied up, and bury toys and small containers of food here to encourage him to use it.

Public responsibility

Before allowing your dog to roam off the lead, check the suitability of the surroundings, making sure he cannot reach any nearby roads or livestock. If he may not come back to you when called, attach a 10-m (30-ft) long training lead to his collar and practise recall training.

🔺 **Digging is a natural, enjoyable activity, so you must divert your dog to a digging pit instead.**

Areas of control

Be sure to keep your dog within your 'area of control': a few metres in wide open spaces to centimetres from your heel in busy areas. You need to assess the following:

- **What** kind of distractions exist around you?

- **Where** are they in relation to you?

- How experienced is your dog at **coping** with them?

- How quickly will he **react** and respond to you?

- How much training have you done to develop **skills**?

Example: If you are walking him in woods, be aware of rabbits and deer that may not be visible but which he can smell ('what'). If the walkway is narrow you know that he could chase an animal before you could intervene, so keep him close to you ('where'). An older dog may be less likely to want to chase ('coping'), and you may have a good rapport with him ('react'). You may also have taught an excellent recall ('skills'). In this case, you can allow him to roam more freely than a less experienced dog.

SKILL
LEVEL

Going on holiday

Whether you travel frequently or only once a year, you still need to think ahead and make arrangements for your dog. He can now accompany you to many dog-friendly hotels, bed-and-breakfasts and rented cottages and apartments both in the UK and Europe. Alternatively, you can arrange for him to stay with family or friends, or put him in kennels, or use a pet-sitting service. Always choose the least stressful option for your dog – he will not understand the human concept of taking holidays.

🔺 **Always microchip your dog as a security measure as this will help reunite you if he ever goes missing.**

Family holidays with your dog

Your dog's companionship on your family holidays is one of the many joys of pet ownership, but it represents a disruption to his normal routine, so anticipate potential problems and find easy solutions. Take him out more frequently for toileting to avoid accidents inside. If you are camping or caravanning, provide him with a secure place, such as his crate, to rest when unsupervised.

Dog-friendly holidays

When you choose your holiday destination, find out in advance where you can go for dog-friendly day trips and meals out. If your dog is not welcome at places you visit, never leave him in your car while you go off exploring or to a restaurant. Dogs can quickly die in cars in hot weather as the interior heats up rapidly, and leaving the window open does very little to reduce the temperature. Active family holidays can be enjoyable for you all if your dog is well equipped for the adventures ahead.

Pet Passports

If you plan to travel abroad with your dog, you must apply for a Pet Passport. This takes time and planning, and the procedures involved must be carried out in the prescribed order with the correct documentation. Your dog will need to be microchipped, vaccinated and blood tested – failure to comply may lead to him being quarantined in your destination country or not being allowed to return home for some time. This is distressing and costly, as vaccinations often require a waiting period before your dog can travel. Go on the DEFRA website and talk to your vet at least eight months in advance before you intend to travel. Also check that your dog is not a banned breed in the country you plan to visit.

🔺 **Crating your dog in the car can provide a safe and secure den as well as preventing him being a distraction and jumping around while you're driving.**

🔺 **Never ever leave your dog unattended in the car. Cars can overheat in seconds causing suffering and even death, on overcast as well as hot, sunny days.**

Boarding kennels

Boarding kennels are the usual option if you're not planning to take your dog on holiday with you. Reputable ones should be licensed by the local authority and must adhere to set standards of cleanliness, warmth and safety. However, they do vary widely in terms of the facilities they provide and the exercise dogs receive. Visit several kennels in your area to get a feel for the experience they offer. Talk to the staff and look at the other dogs staying there. Are they calm and settled or do their pens overlook one another, causing them to bark? What are the feeding and exercise regimes? Note that most kennels will not accept dogs unless their vaccinations are up to date.

Pet sitters

For dogs that rely on routine and feel more secure in their own home, pet sitters are often the best solution. They stay in your house and care for and exercise your dog. This is a particularly good idea if you own several pets.

Checklists

Keep a checklist of things to aim for rather than allowing dog-related tasks to become overwhelming. Here are some simple but essential guidelines to help get you on the right track, as well as things to avoid. Some may take time to accomplish but others are relatively quick and simple. Keep this list to hand and try to complete every point to really achieve what your dog wants.

DO...

- Socialize your puppy from eight weeks onwards until he is at least two years old.
- Take your dog to training classes.
- Learn his body language.
- Get him checked by your vet at least once a year.
- Keep his vaccinations up to date.
- Treat him regularly for worms and fleas.
- Microchip him and keep the records up to date.
- Provide a flat comfortable collar with a visible ID tag.
- Always keep some dog poo bags in your pocket.
- Train your dog to enjoy being handled.
- Keep his coat clean and well groomed.
- Check his teeth regularly and brush them daily.
- Insure him against accidents with third party liability as a minimum.
- Feed him a well-balanced, nutritious diet.
- Neuter your dog or bitch.
- Contact your vet and ask for advice at the first sign of illness or a health problem.
- Make your home secure and dog-proof.
- Keep poisonous substances or choking hazards out of his reach.
- Train your dog to behave calmly in public.
- Teach him an instant sit, recall and not to pull when he's out walking on the lead.
- Exercise him regularly and let him run freely if it is safe.
- Plan where he will stay during holiday periods.
- Contact an accredited pet behaviourist at the first sign of any unusual behaviour.
- Become an expert on your own dog.

DON'T...

- Isolate your dog regularly for long periods.
- Leave him unattended in a parked vehicle.
- Allow him to foul footpaths or public spaces.
- Allow him to walk off the lead near busy roads.
- Allow him to chase livestock, cyclists or joggers.
- Be inconsistent with training your dog or rewarding good behaviour.
- Expect him to remember new skills after just a few training sessions.
- Blame him for not following rules if you have not taught them thoroughly.
- Expect him to understand everything you say.
- Become frustrated with lack of progress.
- Leave him unattended with children or strangers.
- Permit him to race out of the front door.
- Forget to play games with him.
- Allow him to play roughly.
- Allow him to jump on other dogs he does not know.
- Ignore any behaviour problems that may arise.
- Assume he will never bite or show aggressive behaviour.
- Punish him for housetraining accidents.
- Leave it too late before making holiday plans.
- Listen to old wives' tales or unqualified advice.

Socialization checklist

To socialize your puppy or rescue dog effectively, you must ensure that he experiences all the things listed in the table opposite in a safe, positive and enjoyable way. This is an ongoing process that may take many weeks and months, if not years, and you must be committed and keep it up! The most important aspect of socialization is interaction with people and other dogs.

Take proper safety measures at all times and always reward calm, happy behaviour with your attention, tasty treats and praise. If your dog shows signs of uncertainty, reassure him gently and stay composed; distract a puppy with a toy or delicious treat, allowing him more distance next time to ensure you reward a positive response.

Try to make sure that your dog experiences most of the things in each category at least 10 times per week. You can even add your own ideas, depending on where you live and your individual lifestyle. Record your dog's progress by putting a tick in the boxes provided on the chart, or make your own. Stay relaxed but be thorough and vigilant!

People

Adult men and women	☐
Elderly people	☐
Delivery people	☐
Joggers	☐
Cyclists	☐
People in uniform	☐
People in (sun)glasses	☐
Teenagers	☐
Children/toddlers/babies	☐

Other animals

Puppies – quiet/noisy/bouncy	☐
Dogs – dark coat/light coat/big/small	☐
Cats/small pets	☐
Deer/cows/horses/sheep	☐

Environment

1 Out and about

Parks/shops/cafés	☐
School (outside)	☐
Busy roads (on lead)	☐
Vet/groomer/kennels	☐

2 Transport

Cars/lorries/motorcycles/tractors	☐
Trains	☐

3 Surfaces

Smooth/shiny/tiled floor	☐
Grass/gravel/sand	☐

4 Being alone

In a crate/room	☐
Lead held by a stranger	☐

5 Handling

Head/ears/teeth/paws	☐
Lift onto table/gentle restraint	☐

6 Sounds

Hairdryer/vacuum/washing machine	☐
Fridge/dishwasher/central heating/air conditioning	☐
Aeroplane/lawn mower	☐
Telephone/doorbell/answer machine	☐
Fire and smoke alarms	☐
Firework noise	☐
Other barking dogs	☐

Index